Contents

Chapter 1
The Empty Room

*

Animals are such agreeable friends—
they ask no questions, they pass no criticisms.
GEORGE ELIOT

Whenever Jack got home from work, his black lab, Rascal, would rush sliding and slobbering into the front foyer, barking an exuberant welcome. That love and attention made Jack feel like a king.

A sense of calm would sweep over Maria whenever she sat in her favorite chair at night and her Persian cat, Trixie, would jump onto her lap. The TV could be on or off, it didn't matter; Maria could pass the time by just simply petting her purring friend.

Pets fill our lives with joy and companionship. They fill our homes with energy, and they fill our hearts with love.

We hear their unique sounds: purring, whimpering, chittering, squawking, and barking. We see them out of the corner of our eyes, sleeping on their favorite rugs, lapping water from their bowls. And, yes, we smell them. Our homes are permeated with their scents, so much that we hardly notice anymore. They have marked our homes—and us—as their territories. Our floors are dotted with the detritus of pet life: toys, brushes, leashes, and pet beds (not to mention a few carpet stains).

Our schedules have times carved out for our pets—feeding, walking, and cleaning—but there are other moments that just happen. They're always underfoot, brushing against us, leaping on top of us, and bounding into bed with us. They're ready to play even when we aren't, and often they coax us into merriment.

Travis would laugh whenever he found his cat curled up in the kitchen sink, enjoying the drip of the leaky faucet. *Bad kitty!* The counter was off limits. But the sight was so cute and funny that Travis decided to let it slide—and somehow he would always "forget" to get the leak fixed.

Darla would sometimes get annoyed when her dog barked at a rustling tree branch or a passing car, especially in the middle of the night. But she also knew her dog's growly rumblings meant that she was safe. A burglar wouldn't stand a chance.

Pets fill our space with their presence. They keep surprising us. Around any corner, there they are, being themselves, with their steady gaze and simple motives. They can delight us and upset us, but they always bring *life* into our lives. They change us. They bring their particular energy to our existence.

Until they don't anymore.

VACANCY

Understandably, many of us feel devastated by the death of a pet. We may run the gamut of emotions: shock, sorrow, denial, guilt, anger, and then more sorrow. Once the initial shock has worn off, when we've regathered our emotional selves, there's still one feeling that hits us, again and again: emptiness.

Our homes feel empty. We enter a room and receive no fanfare of barking. There are no felines jumping into our laps. We clean up the dog dishes or the litter boxes, the tanks, the cages, and the rubber bones. The smells are sanitized away. And it's quiet. *Too* quiet. No chirping, mewing, growling, or scratching. Even if we still have other pets, we miss the distinct presence of that certain one. In fact, the remaining pets also feel the absence of the lost one. The pets left behind can even show signs of depression. The space just isn't as full as it once was.

Our hearts feel empty too. Pets creep into our affections and curl up there, and when they go, they leave an open space in their exact shape. Life is just not the same without them. Months later, even years later, the emptiness may still yawn inside us. We miss them terribly.

Ron had to put his cat, Gidget, to sleep after a long and difficult illness. Six months later, he was moving out of his condo, putting a few last pieces of furniture in a borrowed pickup truck. Moving one bookcase, Ron saw a little orange ball roll out from underneath. It had been one of Gidget's favorite toys. Ron had to stop working. He broke down in tears, sparking some less-than-sympathetic comments from the guys helping him move.

Our emotional response to the loss of a pet is sometimes complicated because we're not sure what category to put our grief into. No one would blame us for breaking down over the loss of a human we loved, but an animal? Aren't there limits to that grief? The answer is no—we have lost a trusted friend, a confidant, and a family member. Why shouldn't we grieve?

> *Animals are reliable, many full of love, true in their affections, predictable in their actions, grateful and loyal. Difficult standards for people to live up to.*
> Alfred A. Montapert

If you get nothing else from this book (and there's plenty more), get this: *It is normal and natural to grieve over the loss of a beloved pet.* Your tears are nothing to apologize for. Your sorrow is a fitting tribute to a being who you loved. You have deeply invested your emotions in the life of this dear pet, and now you need to respond emotionally to its death.

In chapter 3, we'll look more closely at the grieving process and how to move healthily through it. But don't let anyone tell you that sorrow over your pet is inappropriate or over-the-top. Only you know the shape and size of that empty space within you.

What Grieving Looks Like

Grief can affect your life in any of the following ways.

Physical: You might lose your appetite or feel nauseous. Some people find it hard to sleep. Or perhaps you feel aches and pains in your body.

Emotional: You might find yourself crying at the drop of a hat. Your self-esteem may sag. You also might be sensitive to feelings of guilt, anger, or impatience—even if the situation has nothing to do with your pet.

Psychological: You might forget that your pet is gone and mistakenly set out food or call for it. Perhaps you imagine you hear your pet's sounds or catch a glimpse of your pet out of the corner of your eye. You might want to keep your pet's things around the house for quite a while—or feel a sudden impulse to trash it all.

Mental: You might find it hard to concentrate. Perhaps you feel that each day just drags along. You might re-evaluate decisions you made in regards to your pet and wonder, *What if I had done things differently?*

Spiritual: You might question long-held beliefs. Perhaps you express anger toward God. You might withdraw from your religious group in some way. Or, conversely, you find yourself becoming more spiritual.

Social: You might withdraw from close relationships, or perhaps you'll rely more heavily on certain people. Some feel a need to busy themselves with social activities as a way to distract themselves from their grief.

Before we move into some of the major issues of pet loss, let's look at what pets mean to us. A great deal of research has been done in this area, establishing the importance of the bond between animals and humans. This will help us understand much more about how the loss of a pet can affect our hearts and lives.

WHAT OUR PETS MEAN TO US

At an assisted-care facility in Colorado Springs, Colorado, one of the health-care professionals often brings her dog to work with her. The elderly residents look forward to these "dog days," and they'll invent excuses to stop by her office to visit her pet. The dog, a labradoodle named Thomas, sometimes roams the halls, and people come out of their apartments to pet him. "Thomas is a big star here," says one of the residents. "We all love him."

This professional is on the cutting-edge of health care. She understands the importance of the bond between animals and humans. For people who are socially marginalized with a limited number of human relationships, the interaction with an animal can be especially healing and healthful. Exciting work is being done; for example, children with disabilities and conditions such as autism have benefited from horseback riding. We've long understood the practical value of "seeing-eye dogs" and other service animals, but now we're seeing the emotional value as well.

Something good is going on when a person and an animal care for each other. It is healthy for both of them.

Companionship

"Kitty got me through a lot of hard times," says Lauree about the cat she had as a teenager. "He would always know when I was upset or sick and would come and just stick by me. One time I was very upset about something, and I was close to being at the end of my rope. It was summertime, so I went to the edge of our property and just sat and cried. Even though I didn't call him, Kitty came and sat with me as if to reassure me that he was there and that I would be okay."

While it's true that we tend to ascribe human emotions to our pets (and they can't say anything to deny it), it's also true that scientists are finding increasing evidence of emotional behavior among animals. Lauree may be not only intuitive but also scientifically accurate when she says Kitty was trying to reassure her. Perhaps you've had similar moments with your pets. Over time, you learn to read their responses, and they learn to read yours. They know when you're upset, and it only makes sense that they would try to help you, if only to allow you to continue to help them.

The best thing about a pet is that he or she is there for you. Pets usually spend time with their owners (although admittedly, some cats play hard-to-get!). Every time you walked the dog, every time your cat fell asleep on your lap, or you were ringing a bell to entertain your budgie, you were building a relationship. You got to know the rhythms of your pet's life and they got to know yours. Both of those rhythms adapted to the other. You and your pet were sharing your lives together. In light of this, it's no surprise that losing such a companion would be a major jolt.

"Oliver and I built a relationship based on trust and companionship," says Diane about the family dog, a shih tzu. "Wherever I went, he went. Oliver quickly became my third child. My family began calling me the 'crazy dog lady,' which was fine with me. My husband learned to plan pet-friendly vacations because I could not bear to leave the dog. Oliver loved to hike during our trips in upstate New York and frolic in the ocean in New Jersey. He was small but mighty. I had no idea just how much a furry little 13-pound dog could imbed himself into my life, my heart, and my family."

"I was amazed how Oliver's passing affected me," elaborates Diane's husband, Steve. "The house truly felt empty. Companion dogs like shih tzus are always around—they love being close to their owners. There was this giant void in the house because he was no longer there. Even the cat noticed it. It's been six weeks since Ollie's passing, and the cat still seems out of sorts. And, admittedly, so are we."

Dogs are our link to paradise. They don't know evil or jealousy or discontent. To sit with a dog on a hillside on a glorious afternoon is to be back in Eden, where doing nothing was not boring—it was peace.

Milan Kundera

Unconditional Love

When two or more people talk with one another, their blood pressures often rise. Why is human conversation so stressful? (Remember, there's both good and bad stress.) It's because we all have many things that worry us, even as we're communicating. *Are you getting your point across? What will the other person think of you? Will they interrupt you before you finish? How does their response connect with what you just said? Should you agree or disagree?* Like human relationships, human conversations are two-way streets, and that introduces a number of potential complications: *If you love them, will they love you back?*

By comparison, pets are easy. But when people interact with animals—grooming, petting, and talking to them—their blood pressures tend to lower. According to recent studies, this stress relief is just one of the health benefits of pet ownership. It also tells us something about the unique relationship we have with pets: Scratch under their chin and they'll purr like a freight train. Play a few rounds of fetch, and they'll love you forever. Granted,

Don't be dismayed at goodbyes.
A farewell is necessary before you can meet
again. And meeting again, after moments or
lifetimes, is certain for those who are friends.

Richard Bach

there are some exceptions. There's the whole alpha-dog thing, cats are notoriously independent, and there are some cases where people just never make a love-connection with their pets. But when it works, it really works. The pet is often devoted to his or her "person."

This unconditional love is hard to beat. After working all day in a "dog eat dog" world, it's nice to come home to a loyal canine. Human relationships are rewarding in their own way, but they can be very stressful—even when they're going well. Relationships with pets provide many of the same benefits with fewer of the challenges.

There's an oft-quoted witticism (that is sometimes credited to French leader Charles de Gaulle) that says, "The more I know people, the more I like my dogs." The phrase may be a bit cynical, but it captures a valid point: People are complicated; pets, not so much.

When you've been loved that simply, that fully, such love is hard to replace.

Touch

One of the most important aspects of pet ownership is touch. Quite simply, our pets generally enjoy being touched and petted, and we benefit from that contact as well. "Touching reduces stress and, combined with gentle talk, creates a feeling of intimacy, closeness, completion," write Alan Beck and Aaron Katcher in their book, *Between Pets and People*.

Unfortunately, interpersonal touching is not always available or appropriate in modern society. Although the degree varies from culture to culture, society in general has become more isolated and people have become more protective. Thanks in particular to the prevalence of online modes of interaction, people can go for days without experiencing any human touch. According to studies, this lack of touch is especially prevalent among men.

That's where pets come in. "A pet may be the only being that a man, trained in the macho code, can touch with affection," say Beck and Katcher. "This suggests that a pet may have a special role as a man's child."

This is certainly not true for everyone, but many of us in modern times are starved for positive, affectionate touching. Pets meet that need.

Play

Pets play, and they invite us to play with them. In this way, they renew our youth. No matter what our age, we become kids again when we wrestle with a pup or play chase-the-string with a kitten. We indulge in pointless fun as a way of connecting with another creature. This is entirely healthy and all too absent from our modern lives.

"All work and no play make Jack a dull boy." That aphorism is played out among Jacks and Jills these days, who devote too many hours to making a fortune and too few to having fun. When we do play something, it's often a competition—a serious effort to

The Health Benefits of Having a Pet

In 1977, a team of researchers at the University of Maryland studied a group of 92 heart patients, looking for social factors that might contribute to the patients' survival and recovery. The researchers asked a wide variety of questions, including whether the patients owned pets. Within the following year, 14 of those patients died (or 15 percent). But the researchers noticed a curious distinction. Of the 53 patients who owned pets, only 3 died (6 percent), while 11 of the 39 patients without pets passed away (28 percent). This suggested to the researchers that pets were good for people's health.

The researchers looked for other factors that might be skewing the data. Was it just that dog owners got good exercise from walking their dogs? No, it was found that the non-dog pet owners had an even higher survival rate. Was it just that healthier people were the ones who chose to own pets? That wasn't it either, as the researchers checked the history of the patients and refuted that idea as well.

While denying that pets were a "miracle drug," the researchers affirmed "that having a pet did indeed improve a patient's chances of surviving and did in some way help the patient to be healthier."

Later studies confirmed the concept. People's blood pressure decreases when there's a pet in the room. Pet owners see doctors less often than other people. And people with pets have lower cholesterol.

come out ahead. Sometimes we isolate ourselves by playing computer games.

Watch an animal at play, and you'll see something entirely different—the sheer joy of physicality. They run and jump and flap and fetch simply because they can. And if they beg you to join them, it's because they want you to share in their simple joy. Once again, pets lead us into health and wholeness.

Our Pets, Our Selves

In the novel *Immortality*, authors Milan Kundera and Peter Kussi describe a character who owned a cat: "She saw in the cat a superb independence, pride, freedom of action, and constancy of charm . . . ; in the cat she saw her paradigm; in the cat she saw herself." Later they add, "The cat became one of the attributes of herself." This character judged her suitors according to how they treated her cat.

To spare oneself from grief at all costs can be achieved only at the price of total detachment, which excludes the ability to experience happiness.

Erich Fromm

The writers have captured a very common dynamic. People have long been known to choose pets that resemble themselves, and sometimes they subtly—and often unconsciously—change their appearance to resemble the pet even more. But often there's a deeper psychological interplay going on. Some owners begin to see their pets as smaller, wilder versions of themselves. Their desires and the pet's desires become interchangeable. "Is Fifi cold? I'll close the window." "Mittens didn't like that man who came to the door." What these people often mean is that *they're* cold, or that *they* don't like the guy—but they express it as the pets' feelings. There's not necessarily anything wrong with this, but it can make it all the harder to lose a pet. Indeed, many pet owners describe the experience as "losing a part of myself."

Our Connection to Natural Life

It can be fascinating to watch animals. The great actress Uta Hagen once wrote about a time when she was acting on Broadway and an alley cat wandered onto the stage with her. She suddenly realized that no one was watching her anymore—all eyes were on the cat. Even though she'd had years of expert training (and the cat presumably had none), everyone was focusing on the animal. Why? Because no one knew what it would do next!

There is a life force teeming within our pets, a power that propels them through the day. It's energizing to watch them. In this way they become more than just our companions, but a connection to nature, a symbol of natural life. They reintroduce us to the wild world around us. We normally do a lot to protect ourselves from that wildness, but our pets, even though they're domesti- cated, throw us a lifeline.

Our Bridge to Others

Pets can often become associated with certain people. It's "Grandpa's dog," even though Grandpa passed away a few years ago, or it's "Suzy's cat," even though she's off at college, and her little sister now cares for it. In this way, some pets become "bridges" to others, connecting us with the memory of people who are absent from our lives.

When such a pet dies, it can feel like a double loss. We mourn the passing of Grandpa's dog, but we also feel that Grandpa has been taken away again.

UNDERSTANDING THE DEPTH

One grieving pet-lover confesses that she recently lost her mother and grandmother, but she didn't mourn for them as intensely as she mourned for her pet. "I am still having trouble understanding why. My grief enveloped me and made me feel like I was suffocating. My heart felt like it was being ripped from my body." Adding to the sorrow was her own sense of guilt: Was her pet really more important to her than her mother and grandmother?

Wise friends reassured her that the relationships were quite different. Her pet had been with her every day and depended on her for everything. It was a different kind of bond. "Our love was unconditional," she says.

As you read this book, remember: It is normal and natural to grieve deeply over the loss of a beloved pet. It might have been difficult to go through this chapter, reading about all the blessings of a relationship with a pet—love, companionship, touch, and play—when those are exactly the things that have been lost. This book isn't meant to depress you but to reassure you. The loss of your pet was not a minor issue, and you need not feel guilty about grieving.

The good news is you will eventually feel better. In order to get through the grief, you need to face up to it. Then you'll start turning the grief into growth. In time, you'll be able to celebrate all that your pet contributed to your life.

> *When someone you love becomes a memory, the memory becomes a treasure.*
> Anonymous

Chapter 2
When It's Time

*An animal's eyes have the power
to speak a great language.*
MARTIN BUBER

Georgie was refusing to eat. Jo noticed that the 21-year-old cat was more lethargic than usual, finding a spot on the floor and hardly moving all day. Something was definitely wrong. They'd been to the vet with Georgie's various ailments in recent months, and Jo knew there wasn't much time left.

"Georgie's an old man now," the vet had said, preparing her for the inevitable. "We can do a few things to keep him going a little longer, but eventually you'll have to let him go. You'll know when it's time."

Jo rescued Georgie as a young neighborhood stray; years later, he remained a bit rough around the edges. Though Georgie required some extra patience, Jo was happy to have his company. Always an indoor-outdoor cat, he would take off on a couple of "vacations" for weeks at a time, then would strut back in as if he'd never been gone. Georgie mellowed as the years went on, and he found a permanent home in Jo's heart. At night he would sleep on her shoulder, cuddling his head against her neck.

There was one earlier health scare when 13-year-old Georgie was diagnosed with a thyroid problem. He was already old for a cat, so Jo was prepared for bad news. Luckily, the vet was able to treat the problem; however, the treatment cost over a thousand dollars. It was a challenge for Jo's budget, but she felt the cost was worth it. After all, she gained eight more years with the cat she loved.

But now Georgie—shaky, thin, and delicate—was moving with difficulty, when he was moving at all. It looked like he was in pain. From the kitchen, Jo heard a thump from the living room. Georgie had tried to jump up onto the couch, a move he had effortlessly made thousands of times, but now he couldn't. He was splayed out on the floor and seemed to be in agony.

Jo knew it was time.

Gathering her beloved pet in her arms, she sat on the couch for an hour, reminiscing. She thanked Georgie for all the joy he had brought to her life. She asked God to take Georgie wherever good companions go. She whispered assurances to her beloved cat— he wouldn't have to suffer much longer—and then she took him to the vet.

An examination confirmed her fears. There would be no miracle cure this time. Georgie was given something for the pain, and then something to stop his heart. Jo was able to stay by his side the entire time.

Jo knew there was no second-guessing her decision—there really was nothing else to be done. Georgie had lived a long, full life, and Jo was very grateful, although also very sad. Spend that many years that close to anyone, and you will miss them terribly.

Jo slept in the guest bedroom that night. She couldn't quite manage the old bed without Georgie on her shoulder.

TOUGH CHOICES

As sorrowful as that time was for Jo she was fortunate in one respect: There was little question about what was the right thing to do. Her cat was old and sick and clearly in pain. It was simply Georgie's time to go. But many pet owners face murkier situations. Perhaps there's a chance that the pet could bounce back to full health, but it would require expensive surgery and a long (and possibly painful) recuperation. Pet lovers, sometimes already in shock over a sudden illness, now must juggle several possibilities to determine the right course of action.

Deb had a big cat named Gus. Just 7 years old, he weighed 17 pounds, but he was as playful as a kitten. When Deb first felt a lump on Gus's hip, she didn't give it much thought, but as time went on, the lump grew larger. She finally took him to the vet and was stunned to learn that Gus had cancer.

Deb was referred to a nearby university veterinary hospital, where Gus was further evaluated. He loved the attention he received from all of his doctors. He was purring so loudly, they couldn't hear his heartbeat! But there was more bad news: It was an extremely aggressive and rare type of cancer that had spread throughout the body. The doctor suggested wide-angle surgery, followed by chemotherapy and periodic MRIs.

The price tag for all this treatment was $5,000 to $10,000—a big problem for Deb, who was struggling to get by on disability and a part-time job. The vet also said that there was only a 10 to 20 percent chance the cat would survive more than a few years even with the treatment. Without treatment, Gus was expected to live about six months.

It was a tough call, but Deb simply did not have the money. "So I took Gus home to die," she says. She read up on homeopathic remedies that could help with his condition. She fed Gus wheat grass, which he loved. "He continued to be a happy, normal cat for the next year and a half. Then I noticed that he was coughing and had started to lose weight. I knew the time had come to put him out of his pain," says Deb. "The veterinary hospital made me an imprint of his paw to keep in remembrance, and I treasure it still. Gus lived much longer than predicted, and I like to think that I made his short life as happy as possible."

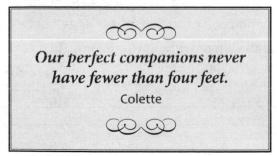

Our perfect companions never have fewer than four feet.
Colette

Euthanasia: Things to Consider

● **What are the odds?** Many people find veterinarians even more forthcoming than their own physicians when it comes to discussing various treatment options. You'll hear possibilities and percentages. Of course, these are educated guesses—no one can know exactly how your pet would respond, but the information provided can help pet owners weigh the options. Don't be afraid to ask your vet questions.

● **Current quality of life.** Sometimes there's nothing to be done for the ailing pet, and it becomes a matter of time. Consider your pet's quality of life during this time: Is the pet in pain or discomfort now? Is it losing control over its functions? Does this ailment make the pet difficult to live with?

● **Quality of life during and after treatment.** Perhaps there is something that can be done to prolong the life of your pet. Surgery certainly isn't fun for anyone, and a lengthy recuperation period can be frustrating and even painful for your pet. What will your pet's life be like if it can't walk or run, or if it can't do other things it once enjoyed?

● **Life span with or without treatment.** The vet should be able to give you an educated guess, but it's no guarantee. Given the pet's age, how long would you expect it to live even if a treatment were successful?

● **Your economic situation.** There is no shame in recognizing your financial limitations. What is the estimated cost of the treatment and necessary care? If you use the money for surgery or other treatment, what will it mean for your own or your family's financial future?

In terms of your financial situation, how would you describe the possibility of further care for your pet?

___ *Impossible*
___ *Would set us back financially for many years*
___ *A big stretch, but we could recover*
___ *Affordable*

● **Your emotional state.** It is certainly emotionally difficult to deal with the death of your pet, but it might also be tough to handle a lengthy period of uncertainty as your pet struggles to recover from an illness.

● **Your family.** Consider how the options presented to you will impact the whole household, including children and any other animals you may have. Will you have to focus all your attention on one pet, to the detriment of others in your home? Do you need to confer with other family members to make this decision? If so, contact them and get the discussion going.

● **If you do opt for euthanasia...** Who needs to say goodbye to the pet? How can you give them that opportunity?

When we're talking about life, death, and love, money shouldn't enter into the discussion, should it? But of course it does. Even so, how can you put a price on the life of a pet you love dearly? Simply put, you can't, but money is one of several factors to consider when facing such a choice. The wise and caring pet owner will take all of these into account.

A LOSE-LOSE SITUATION

Many people have struggled with this decision to euthanize their pets, and a good many of them later feel guilty, or perhaps second-guess themselves. *What if I had more money to spend on treatment? What if we took a chance on an experimental procedure? Maybe my pet would have bounced back on its own.*

There may be some second-guessing, but more often than not, the difficult decision they made is the right one. Vets generally give thorough, well-informed information to pet owners, who tend to have an intuitive sense of their pets' pain. The factors mentioned above—money, expectations, emotions—might not be quantifiable on a spreadsheet, but they're part of the decision-making process.

"A risk-reward rationale comes into play," says psychologist Thomas Whiteman, who has also been through this difficult situation with a pet. "You have to weigh the benefits and costs of the different options." While it may seem inappropriate to be so mathematical about the life of your treasured companion, you have to acknowledge a 20 percent chance is different from an 80 percent chance. You may want to cling to any hope of your pet's recovery and survival, but you also need to face reality: Is a slim chance of success worth the risk? What's more, would your pet really want to go through that experience, given the long odds against its success?

It may feel like a lose-lose situation. Few congratulate themselves on making a good choice in the matter, but many pet owners—advised by caring veterinarians—get a sense of what they need to do, whether it's taking a chance on a medical procedure, putting the pet to sleep, or waiting a bit longer. You may still second-guess your decision, but as long as you have the pet's best interests in mind, it's hard to make a bad choice.

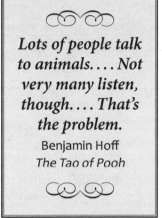

Lots of people talk to animals.... Not very many listen, though.... That's the problem.
Benjamin Hoff
The Tao of Pooh

The Association for Pet Loss and Bereavement notes on its website, "Most people later worry that they finally opted to do this too late—or too soon. Rarely do we meet with a client who feels this was done at the right time.... they are now experiencing what we commonly refer to as euthanasia remorse. The decision was not theirs anymore. It had been taken away from them by the terrible illness. Actually, there was no longer any decision to make. It simply had to be that way."

"It was *extremely* difficult," says one woman who had gone through this experience with her dog, an Oriental shorthair.

"My vet twice suggested that I needed to let [the dog] go, and I canceled both appointments. In the end, my dog had lost half his body weight and was on all types of meds including appetite stimulants. However, the ulcers in his mouth were so bad it was impossible for him to eat. The day he could not jump and fell was the day I made the hardest decision of my life—to let him go."

A while back, a wise friend told her that when the dog was ready to go, he would let her know. As it happened, she sat in the car outside the vet's office, telling her dog it would be the last time they would ever need to go there. "To my utter shock, he reached out of his carrier and put his paw on my hand, as if he was saying, 'It's okay. I'm ready now.'"

REALITY CHECK

We often like to think of our pets in "people" terms, attributing to them human thoughts and emotions, but, of course, they're not human. It's impossible to know exactly what goes on in their minds, and we can't assume that they approach the end of life the same way we do.

"Our pets do not get upset or sentimental at the prospect of their own death," writes bereavement counselor Wallace Sife in *The Loss of a Pet*. "That is a projection of our own fear... We should not torture ourselves during our grief by agonizing about this and distorting the final memories of our beloved companion animals."

The animal world is, in a word, beastly. Pain and death are part of life. In a way, by domesticating our pets, protecting and providing for them, we remove them from the dangers of the wild. We take responsibility for them, which we exercise in many ways during their lives. That care extends to medical treatment, which of course would not be available to them in the wild. We extend their life by bringing them into our homes, and when it seems that there is nothing left for them but great pain, we ease their death. This is also part of the responsibility we take on as pet owners and caregivers.

Most pets have short lives, compared to our own. It may not be something we want to think about, but the truth is that we take on the responsibility of pet ownership knowing that, at some point, we'll have to say goodbye.

"Pets are with us such a short time," says animal rescue expert Jennifer Wesh, "and yet just long enough to make it through milestones with us—graduations, losses, marriages, babies, breakups, new jobs, etc. They are there to see us through those things, and they are a part of those things."

*Although it's difficult today
to see beyond the sorrow,
May looking back in memory
help comfort you tomorrow.*

Anonymous

Given the transitory nature of our pets' lives, it should come as no surprise that it's likely we'll have to say an all-too-early goodbye to our beloved pets. Yet knowing that doesn't make it any easier. This realization should help us put the emphasis on quality of life rather than quantity. In regards to a pet, we should not only be asking ourselves, "Can it live a little longer?" but also, "How long can it live a good life?" The miracles of modern science can help keep a pet alive for a few more months or years than it normally would, but we must consider what kind of life the pet would live in that time. If the future holds only pain and more disease, it makes sense to put the pet to sleep. "It's probably one of the nicest things we're able to do for our pets," says Wesh.

To every thing there is a season, and a time to every purpose under heaven: a time to be born and a time to die.

Ecclesiastes 3:1

Often our desire to extend our pets' lives comes from our own sense of shock. We may know that this day will come, but we're never ready for it. And since animals are not able to verbalize the aches and pains that may signal the onset of a disease, often their physical symptoms will seem to come on suddenly. No matter how well you think you know your pet, it's hard to catch all the nuances. Many pet owners talk about their surprise when their animals suddenly stop eating or can't walk. The vet's examination might reveal an internal problem that had been brewing for months and is now out of control. In such a case, you might blame yourself for not being more vigilant or for not noticing the problem in time, but that's not reasonable. It is simply the nature of things that pets cannot tell us their problems as they develop. Some animals instinctively hide their symptoms. No matter how watchful we are, we will always be at the mercy of these "sudden" ailments.

Even when we're still reeling in shock from the turn of events, we may have to make difficult choices about putting the pet to sleep. The first stage of grief is denial, so it makes sense that of course we want to avoid all discussion of death. Let the vet fix the problem, make the pet good as new, and then we can all act as if this never happened. It's sobering when we learn this isn't possible.

If you've already been in this situation, you've been through an emotional wringer. As you begin the process of emotional recovery, you might be feeling guilt and regret. *If only I had seen it sooner. Did I make the right choice? What should I have done differently?*

Although it may be difficult, try to let go of these nagging questions. As we've seen, the choice of putting a pet down or continuing with treatment has many variables, and that includes your emotional state and the pet's well being. There's no perfect answer. Perhaps you had to make a momentous decision in a rather short time, when you were still reeling from the initial news of your pet's problem. You had a lot of issues to weigh; you weighed them, and then you made a choice. *Whatever that choice was*, it was a loving act of a responsible caretaker.

IN THE ROOM

"She didn't mind going to the vet," says Amelia about her 13-year-old German shepherd. "So when we got there, she just went in the exam room. I was crying so hard, I decided I could not stay with her. I don't know to this day if that was the wrong decision, but I can still picture her face looking at me when I walked out of the room."

Of course that moment is a highly emotional one. Vets often give pet owners the opportunity to stay in the room and even cradle the animal while the final injections are given. Some owners choose to do this and some choose not to. Those who don't stay in the room often feel some guilt afterward.

"I'm a coward!" exclaims one woman, who has had several dogs over the years. "I can never be with them as they leave this world. It hurts too much."

If you feel bad about leaving your pet before the very end, remember that you are or were dealing with several different factors in making that decision. Amelia was facing a situation where her dog was carefree, but she was a basket case. If she was bawling in the dog's final moments, it might have upset the dog. By leaving, she allowed the dog to remain peaceful in a place it enjoyed, right up to the end.

It's all too easy to second-guess your decisions regarding your pet's health care and euthanasia. The stress involved with making these choices may leave you feeling especially vulnerable, but cut yourself a break. Trust that you made a legitimate choice during a difficult time. Your pet would certainly not blame you.

FAMILY FAREWELLS

As a boy, Ted adopted a dog that literally followed him home from school. He and Duke were inseparable as they grew up together. When Ted went to college 1,000 miles away, he left Duke, a mid-size springer spaniel, in the capable care of his mother.

Dogs' lives are too short. Their only fault, really.

Kahlil Gibran

A few years later, while Ted was still in college, he got a call from his mother: Duke had been seriously ill, and they had to put him to sleep. "I remember thinking, 'Was there something more they could have done?'" Ted says. "I was a little angry at my parents for not calling me sooner. I'm not sure what I could have done, but I still felt he was *my* dog. I wanted a chance to say goodbye."

Fast-forward a few decades. Ted was married with three kids of his own. The family got a small black cockapoo they named Max. This was not the "manly" dog Ted originally wanted, but his wife loved little Max, and so did the kids. Eventually Ted began to take Max jogging, and he loved the way Max welcomed him home from work.

"Every day Max greeted me at the door," Ted says. Then one day he found Max lying under the coffee table, alive but lethargic, his

Some Final Thoughts

Here are some things to consider when making an end-of-life decision for your pet.

___ **Ask questions.** Know the choices, the chances, and the vet's recommendation.

___ **Can you be with your pet at the end?** Do you want to?

___ **Should you get the whole family involved?** Would they want to be involved? How would you do this?

___ **Be realistic about money.** How much can you really afford for treatment?

___ **Do you need some final moments with your pet?** What will you say or do?

. . . and after the decision has been made:

___ **Let it rest.** Fight the urge to go back through pro-and-con arguments.

___ **Cry.** You're not mourning the decision, but the situation that made the decision necessary.

___ **Comfort one another.** Especially if there were several people involved in the decision, you'll need to affirm each other in this difficult choice.

___ **Tell those closest to both you and the pet.** Make these calls as a way of honoring their relationship with the pet and mobilizing emotional support for you.

stomach distended. A quick trip to the vet found that an internal tumor had burst. Medication could perk up the dog for an hour or so, but he would die that day without an operation. Even with the expensive surgery, it was a 50–50 proposition; at best Max would probably live only another year. Ted and his wife decided against the operation.

Remembering his own issues with his boyhood dog's death, Ted tried to get his kids to the vet's office to say goodbye to the family pet. One was in high school, and he arrived quickly, but the other two were attending a nearby college. Ted left them frantic messages, but they didn't receive them in time.

Ted, his wife, and son were able to hold Max as he went to sleep for the final time. "I'm glad we got to do that," he says. Unfortunately, his two oldest children never had that closure, and they still seem to hold some pain and anger about Max's death.

The loss of a pet is hard on any family, but there can be extra resentment when a decision is made to put a pet to sleep. Someone has to make that decision, and that person sometimes has to bear the brunt of family members second-guessing his or her decision. This questioning, often with an underlying anger, is not always rational. It's born from the pain of loss. Ted admits now that his resentment toward his mother

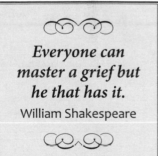

> *Everyone can master a grief but he that has it.*
> William Shakespeare

was ill-founded, since he had been out of the dog's life for several years. Maybe someday his kids will realize that he did his best to include them, but no one wanted to extend Max's pain any longer.

If your family is bristling with issues like this, try to talk about it. If that doesn't work, wait a few months and revisit the issue again. Eventually, as people see the whole truth of the matter, the anger should dissipate. After all, decisions had to be made—quickly and perhaps not perfectly—but they were made with the most loving of intentions for everyone involved.

I hold it true, whate'er befall;
I feel it, when I sorrow most;
'Tis better to have loved and lost
Than never to have loved at all.
Alfred Lord Tennyson

Chapter 3
Healing Happens

—✳—

"Heartbreak is life educating us."
GEORGE BERNARD SHAW

"I was totally lost. I had a hole in my heart and my life."

"When she passed away in my arms, I felt like a hammer hit me in the stomach. I ached and could barely breathe. I cried constantly for about a week."

"When I lose a pet, I feel like I have lost my heart. There is no way to console me, no way to comfort me."

"I remember waking up the next morning, and the first thing I saw was a picture I'd made of him. I burst into tears."

"I felt like my joy was gone. She was my light, she made me special. She loved me. It feels lonely and quiet without her voice."

"The inconsolable grief I felt was indescribable. It lasted two days. I had no idea it'd be so intense. I continue to grieve every day, but with each passing day the grief becomes more manageable."

"I got very angry because I could not believe my baby was gone. I am in that stage right now. I cannot look at pictures of her or see her stuff."

"My pet has been gone for years. I still cannot speak to a person about him without choking up."

You've been there, haven't you? Or perhaps you're still there, caught in the fresh experience of grief. This book does not aim to cheer you up or to banish your sadness. The fact is, crying is something many people need to do as part of their healthy grieving process. This chapter will help you to understand your emotional responses.

In grief, it is important to remember that:

- You are not going crazy, though it might feel like that.

- It is not "silly" to mourn the death of an animal, no matter what some insensitive friends might say.

- You don't need to immediately get a new pet. You might choose to do so at some point, but there's no need to rush it.

- It is not abnormal to feel deep sadness even a year after your pet's passing.

- Feelings of guilt and anger are common but usually groundless. (Be careful not to damage human relationships you need for support in this difficult period.)

- Time does heal emotional wounds, but not automatically. You need to participate in your own healing.

- The best way to heal is to feel your feelings. Don't stifle them.

- Feel *today's* feelings. Don't try to feel the way you think you should be feeling a year from now. Be patient with the process.

STAGES OF GRIEF, PART ONE

In 1969, psychiatrist Dr. Elisabeth Kübler-Ross gave the counseling world a great gift with her seminal book *On Death and Dying*. As she studied terminally ill patients, she recognized a process that occurred as they struggled to deal with their illnesses and mortality. At first, the patients couldn't believe their prognoses, and they tried to act as if it weren't true. As they began to accept reality, they would often become angry—with themselves, at the doctors, at loved ones, at God, or even at the disease. This would lead to an energetic period in which they would try to beat the

When you are sorrowful look again in your heart, and you shall see that in truth you are weeping for that which has been your delight.

Kahlil Gibran

disease by means of aggressive treatment, radical lifestyle changes, and prayer. When these efforts failed, the patients would typically lose energy and become very sad. There was nothing to be done. Finally, at the depths of this malaise, some patients would find a strange kind of calm, as they finally accepted what was happening to them and tried to make the best of it.

In essence, Kübler-Ross identified what she called the five stages of grief: denial, anger, bargaining, depression, and acceptance. In the years since, counselors have applied these stages to bereavement, addiction, divorce, and virtually any upheaval in life. In general, the model fits a wide range of human experiences. Some have tried to place timelines on the different stages—if you were divorced a year ago, you still have six months of depression left—but this sort of math is fraught with difficulty. While the stages of grief identify a general pattern, each person is different, and each crisis is different. The stages don't run like clockwork.

Observers have also found that the stages don't always proceed in a certain order. In fact, some people will show signs of all five stages on the same day. Other times, stages may lie dormant within the psyche until you experience something that triggers that stage and its related emotions. For example, someone cuts you off on the highway, and suddenly you're feeling every bit of anger you've stored up for the past six months—not just at that driver, but at your parents, at the IRS, at your losing sports team, at the companies that make the lids of pickle jars too tight, and at your vet for not finding the problem with your pet sooner.

When you're in that mind frame, it certainly doesn't matter whether the anger is totally misplaced or not.

The same can be said for any stage. Ted, who used to go jogging with his little dog, still finds himself calling for Max when it's time to run—and it's been a year since Max died. You might have a vivid dream of your pet and awake expecting to find it beside you. Our minds play tricks of denial on us, as a way of delaying our new reality or hanging onto the old one.

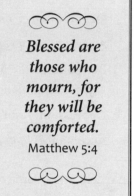

> *Blessed are those who mourn, for they will be comforted.*
> Matthew 5:4

Kübler-Ross said that the stages she identified were "never meant to help tuck messy emotions into neat packages," so be wary of anyone who tells you how you should feel at any point in the grieving process. Emotions *are* messy; sometimes we revisit a stage we thought we were done with. This is normal too. With that said, the stages of grief can help us to understand the general process, the sort of journey our emotions take as they come to terms with loss.

STAGES OF GRIEF, PART TWO

In the decades since Kübler-Ross's groundbreaking observations, others have tried to tweak the model or present entirely new ways of looking at grief. Some experts have suggested that one who grieves is really doing two different things: letting go of what's lost and building a new life without it. Some experts talk about "integration" of one's memories into the fabric of a new life; we want to move forward but we also search for a way to carry what we've lost. As we grieve, we're constantly dealing with both the past and the future.

We can see this double dynamic in the classic Kübler-Ross model:

Denial: *I can go on as if this never happened.*

Anger: *I can't go on because I'm hurt and upset.*

Bargaining: *Maybe I can find a way to fix things quickly and move on.*

Depression: *I can't go on because the sorrow is too great.*

Acceptance: *I am able to go on even though this happened.*

In recent years, some experts have tucked two additional stages into the classic model. In the first of these new stages, denial is broken down into feelings of pain and guilt. The other stage, wedged in between depression and acceptance, is one in which people try to rebuild their lives. Let's go through these "seven stages of grief" and see how they apply specifically to the loss of a pet. Keep in mind, however, that this is not an agenda or a schedule. It's a general observation of how many people process grief. You may see yourself in these descriptions, but don't be alarmed if you don't. Your grieving experience is unique.

Stage 1: Shock and Denial

This can begin the first moment you recognize a problem. Maybe you feel a lump under your pet's skin or you notice a limp. You don't want to deal with a problem, so you tell yourself it doesn't exist. Denial can also occur at several points thereafter. Although the vet explains that there's a minimal chance of survival, you don't really take it in—you're confident that your pet will defy the odds.

Or perhaps the death was sudden and unexpected, and you simply can't accept that it happened. Expected or not, even after a pet's death, some owners continue to live as if he or she were still with them, keeping the pet's belongings around, perhaps even keeping the water bowl fresh. It's difficult for them to give in to the reality of the loss.

The addition of shock to the denial stage is very helpful, because these feelings aren't just mind games. With the loss of a pet, especially if it's a sudden death, you might find it difficult to function, walking around in a daze. People in this stage often seem disengaged from life.

Give sorrow words; the grief that does not speak whispers the o'er-fraught heart and bids it break.
William Shakespeare

Why does this happen? When the human body sustains an injury, it responds with numbness in the area of the injury and some-times a general state of shock. This is because when the body can't deal with pain, it temporarily shuts down its pain receptors. It's a survival mechanism. The same sort of thing happens with our emotions when we face a painful loss. We disengage temporarily from the world that has brought us this pain.

This is perfectly normal. But in some cases, a person's denial goes on too long or the shock strikes too deep, and it keeps that person from normal functioning. However, if denial and shock are temporary symptoms, it's typically nothing to worry about.

Stage 2: Pain and Guilt

It is not uncommon for someone to cry steadily for two or three days after losing a beloved pet. This too is a healthy expression of the pain of loss. Thoughts and regrets rapidly crash through one's mind as you "wake up" from your denial. Numbness is wearing off; your emotions are extraordinarily raw. Any little reminder can set you off on another crying jag.

One thing that intensifies the sorrow is that, in previous times of grief, you've had your pet there for comfort, and now you don't. "You're never really alone when you have a pet. Whether you come in super excited and dancing around over an awesome first date or when you're chest-deep in tissues over the loss of a family member, your pet is there in times when there is absolutely no way you'd want another person to see you," says animal rescuer

Jennifer Wesh. "They know us in a way no one else does, and that is why that relationship and bond is so hard to lose."

In many cases, added to the sorrow is a sense of guilt. It can be easy to find reasons to blame yourself (whether it's rational or not). You think of all the things you could have done differently. Perhaps you wonder what your pet thought of you in its final moments, or you worry that your actions made things worse for your family. You even blame yourself for crying too much—which makes you cry more. This blame game can become a vicious cycle.

Stage 3: Anger

Anger often arises over a sense of injustice, toward yourself or someone else. In anger you feel that you don't deserve this, and your pet certainly didn't deserve this. Anger can turn this way and that, seeking someone to blame. As with the guilt in the previous stage, anger is not always rational. You feel like you want to lash out. Perhaps you get mad at the veterinarian for not trying harder. Or maybe it's another family member for falling short in their responsibility toward the pet. It's not uncommon for people to express their anger toward God in these moments.

It's even possible that you will become angry at your pet for leaving you. This is especially true in a situation where the pet is missing, ran off into traffic, or when the animal has just become ill. You blame the pet, and then you blame yourself for blaming the innocent pet.

What to Do with Your Anger

It surprises some people when their grief erupts into anger. They find themselves lashing out at people for no good reason. While anger is a natural part of the grieving process, it can also do some damage if not managed well.

Bottling up anger can hurt you physically and emotionally. Here are some ways to effectively handle your anger.

Gather Your Team. Let your family and closest friends know how you're feeling. Apologize in advance for outbursts of anger that might be launched in their direction.

Focus Your Feelings. Anger tends to be scattershot, imprecise in choosing its target, so take some time to focus on what you're really angry at: the disease, the power of death, or the forces of nature. You might even invite your "team" to join you in yelling at this true foe.

Get Your Body into It. Work out, go jogging, or hit a punching bag. Let your anger fuel each move. This is a classic way to "get it out of your system." Some people have expressed their anger by throwing old dishes against a backyard tree or pummeling an old sofa. One guy took the opportunity to tear down a wall in his basement—a job that had been on his to-do list for some time, but now he had the energy for it.

Turn It Positive. Take this angry energy and do something good for society, or for other animals. Perhaps you can organize a charitable event to benefit your local animal shelter in honor of your departed pet.

Often this anger revolves around yourself, and you get a second helping of guilt. Why didn't you use your X-ray vision to see that tumor before it grew? Why don't you earn enough money to pay for the expensive operation that had a slight chance of saving your pet's life? It might not make sense, but you are heated up, and you need to fire away at someone.

> *Hope comes as a ray of sun amidst the cold, dark rain, moving us into the light where love can heal our pain.*
> Anonymous

The danger in the anger stage is that you will do something foolish and drive people away from you. There have been marriages that have broken up in the aftermath of a pet's death. There have been lawsuits filed against innocent veterinarians. And there have been millions of harsh words uttered against people who don't deserve them.

Stage 4: Bargaining

This stage is often the hardest to understand. Your main motive in the bargaining stage is to fix the problem as fast as possible. You want to stop feeling such sadness, and so you reach for a quick cure. If you get to this stage while your pet is still alive, this is where you push for the experimental operation that will hopefully make everything all better. For those whose pets have died, their instinct might be to run out and get a new pet just like the old one, expecting that this would set things right again.

Of course that's not the answer. Grief is something you work through over time; there's no way to magically beam yourself out of it. Another pet might be a great idea eventually, but you know that no creature can fully replace the one you've lost. You still have to go through the experience of loss.

In the bargaining stage, people are especially susceptible to escapist addictions. If they have issues with drugs or alcohol, they may be tempted to "medicate" their grief in these ways. Others distract themselves from their grief with behavioral addictions, including gambling, shopping, or sex. These attempts to shut down the sadness may work in the short term, but the normal feelings of loss will inevitably creep up again.

On a positive note, bargaining is an attempt to deal with the reality of the loss and to get back to "normal" in some sense. The problem is often in the griever's lack of patience—the "quick fix" mentality won't really fix anything, and it could get you into even more trouble.

Stage 5: Depression

Well, if a quick fix won't work, what will? When you reach the stage of depression, you finally realize that life can't go back to the way it was. What's lost is lost. You feel powerless to change anything about your situation, and you're stuck in your sadness.

This stage can often resemble the shock of the first stage of denial as you wander around with little energy to do anything useful. It may also feel a lot like the sorrow of the second stage of guilt as

Callous Comforters

Some people just don't get it. "It's only a pet," they say. "Why are you so upset? Just get a new one." As if this precious creature were some *thing*, some commodity.

"Comforters" like this may mean well, but they completely fail the sensitivity test. You could try to re-educate them, but it may be a waste of time. If they truly want to listen, you may tell them what your pet meant to you. But it's also fine to say, "Thanks for your concern," and walk away. You have limited resources in this time of grief, so pick your battles.

Of course walking away might not be an option if the "callous comforter" is part of your family, or even your spouse. If this is the case, you'll need to ask for more consideration. Understand where they're coming from, but ask them to consider your situation as well. "This might seem strange to you, but this pet was a very dear friend to me. The loss has affected me deeply. Even if you don't understand it, please give me time and space to grieve for my friend."

You might have to coach people on how to comfort you. You might even want to share with them books like this one. Try not to resent them if they never quite get it—after all, what you're going through may simply be out of their realm of experience.

you cry yourself to sleep each night. But this sorrow runs deeper. It exposes a deep sense of emptiness. You're not enjoying the things you used to; you barely can taste the foods you love. You may feel like you have no more emotional resources to cope with the loss. Obviously, this stage is not enjoyable, but this is where you "hit bottom"—and you must bottom out in order to move upward again. You *will* heal from this ordeal.

Stage 6: Testing and Reconstruction

In Kübler-Ross's original model, depression gave way to acceptance. For many people, this transformation was so sudden that it felt almost magical: They woke up one morning and literally smelled the coffee. It's as if their quota of grieving had been met and they could begin to enjoy life again.

But newer paradigms reflect a different reality as many people continue to function as the "walking wounded." For them, there isn't a sudden moment where the gray skies turn blue. Instead,

Many who have spent a lifetime in it can tell us less of love than the child that lost a dog yesterday.
Thornton Wilder

they gradually begin to put their lives back together. They start doing things with people again, rather than rushing home to hibernate. They allow themselves to have a little fun. This is a testing process, and there is some trial-and-error. Painful memories may resurface at any time, driving them back to their private grieving. Still, they're slowly rebuilding.

Stage 7: Acceptance

First, let's discuss what acceptance does *not* mean. It doesn't mean the beloved pet is forgotten. It doesn't mean that the mourner is glad that the pet is gone. It doesn't mean the person won't still burst into tears now and then. The key here is that in this stage, the person integrates the loss into his or her life. The memory of the pet is carried along as the person moves into new adventures.

There might always be a sense of sadness over the loss, but this is matched and exceeded by a sense of gratitude for the time they were able to have with the pet. They might wonder if they'll ever see their pet again in some future heaven, but they're not consumed by this thought. They step forward into robust earthly lives, confident it's what their dear, departed pet would want them to do.

NAVIGATING THE STAGES

People always want to know how long the grieving process lasts. The answer is, "As long as it takes." It may be frustrating, but there's no way of knowing—it may take a few days, a few months, or a few years. It's simply not helpful or realistic to set up timetables.

When a Pet Goes Missing

The grieving process looks different when a pet goes missing. Basically, you don't know when to begin grieving. There's the initial shock of realizing the pet's gone, and perhaps some early denial ("It'll come back tomorrow"). Once you realize it's really gone, then there's a flurry of activity—searching high and low, posting signs in the community, alerting the authorities, and checking with local shelters. These attempts can resemble the stage of bargaining, except that they're not a "quick fix," but solid attempts to solve the problem.

There is some sadness in this time and even some anger, but the emotional focus is on hoping for the return of the pet. But with each passing day, the outlook grows dimmer. You go from optimism to realism to pessimism. How long before you conclude that the pet is gone for good? There are plenty of stories of pets that wandered off for two or three weeks and then reappeared. When can you legitimately start grieving?

In cases like this, the grieving process becomes messier. With each day the chance of a safe return gets slimmer, and so each day sees a combination of denial, pain, anger, and "bargaining" activities, until you give up hope. For some, the lack of closure is especially hard to deal with. They'd rather know for certain the status of their pet, even if it were bad news. Others might feel strangely comforted by the thought that the pet may still be alive. Their sadness is lessened as they realize that the pet is probably, but not necessarily, gone for good.

Your unique situation will require a unique journey through some, if not all, of the stages. It will take as long as it needs to.

There's one thing about this journey, however: You can't rush it. If you don't spend enough time in a particular stage, chances are you'll bounce back to it later. The grieving process is like the IRS: It must get its due.

Complicated Grieving

There are, however, some complicating factors that can extend the grieving process.

- **When the person feels strong guilt over the pet's death.** People can generally deal with the "phantom guilt" that accompanies a loss ("I should have done more sooner"), but if they feel their actions or negligence directly caused the pet's death, the early stages of grief may take longer.

- **When the attachment to the animal is especially strong.** In this case, we're talking about not just love for the pet but a practical or emotional dependency. This would be true in the case of service animals, and in other situations where the person's life has revolved around the pet. It will take longer to reconstruct one's life without such a pet in it.

- **When the pet was associated with another person.** If the pet serves as a reminder of, say, a departed spouse or a distant child who used to care for it, then the task of grieving doubles, for you're not only mourning the pet but also the person.

- **When the loss was especially traumatic.** A sudden shock, a gruesome accident—these can keep a person at the denial stage for longer than usual.

- **When the person has few other friends or family for support.** It's very hard to reconstruct a life without the pet, when the pet was all that mattered. Supportive friends keep grieving people moving through the stages, and they're a crucial component of the reconstruction process that frequently pulls a griever out of depression. A person can certainly get through the grief without any outside support; it simply may take a bit longer.

Whether or not these extenuating circumstances apply to your situation, it's essential to realize that healing takes time. Just as a broken bone or a scraped knee requires a certain period of recuperation, so does a heart broken by the loss of a dear companion.

Take all the time you need.

Chapter 4

Recovering, Reformatting, and Replacing

I thought I could describe a state;
make a map of sorrow. Sorrow, however,
turns out to be not a state but a process.
It needs not a map but a history.

C. S. LEWIS

"By the time we realized how sick Frankie was, it was too late," says Lynette about the cat she got when she was 12. It was just a year later that he started having health problems. "We took him to the vet's office and left him there. He died there the next day."

Lynette was very upset, and took her anger out on those closest to her. "You're probably glad he died," she told her mother. "You never liked him anyway."

A crisis brings out utterances and feelings we normally keep quiet. At the time, Lynette felt she had good reason to suspect this. She had received Frankie as a gift from a friend, and her mother had never been very excited about it. Grudgingly she had allowed the cat to stay, but its care was entirely Lynette's responsibility, and it was never allowed to enter Mom's room.

Now the pain of losing her pet worsened the already difficult relationship Lynette had at the time with her mother. In her darker moments, she suspected her mother of poisoning the cat, a charge which she now, years later, admits was groundless.

"At the time, my life was pretty bad. I was in eighth grade and that whole experience was nasty. My parents were close to divorcing, and I think my mom and sister were also having issues, so even before Frankie died, there weren't many positives going on. Losing the cat was a big blow," says Lynette. "I cried myself to sleep a lot—over the cat's death, but also because of how miserable my mother was in general as a result of everything else going on in her life."

Owning a pet doesn't occur in a vacuum. There is a life you are living, with friends and neighbors, with jobs and responsibilities, with bills to pay and appointments to keep. A pet becomes a part of that broader life. Perhaps the whole family enjoys the pet together, or friends come over and greet your pet even before they greet you. But there are other times when your pet provides a refuge from the harsh realities of life. This was certainly the case with Lynette, and when Frankie died, she felt she didn't have much of a life to go back to.

"Pets to us are purity," says Dr. Donna Alberici, a professor of psychology. "They never tell us we look bad. They're always happy to see us. When my pet 'waves' to me, it's all for me."

Alberici notes that there's a kind of "perfection" in this relationship. "We grant attributes to them that we don't give to humans." We see our pets as perfectly loyal, perfectly supportive—and when there's a lack of loyalty or support in the world around us, this is especially important.

Psychologist Thomas Whiteman talks about the "bonding" between a pet and its owner. "It's possible for someone to own a pet and not bond with it, but when there is a connection made, it's very positive. They communicate with you, but not with words."

> *Look thoroughly into yourself. There is a fountain of strength that will spring up whenever you look there.*
>
> Marcus Aurelius, *Antisthenes*

In this way, pets "say" exactly what we need to hear, especially when we're feeling emotionally needy. We're grateful for their support, idealizing them as the perfect friends. "With other people, we have a mixture of good and bad memories," Whiteman says, "but there are only pleasant memories with pets."

He notes that this is especially important for single people or senior citizens who may not have much human companionship. A pet provides much-needed support in these social situations, and when that pet passes on, the grief can be overwhelming.

Under these circumstances, grieving becomes even more difficult. It's not just about "getting over" an emotional loss; it means reconstructing your life, a post-pet existence in which support must come from somewhere else. It also requires a certain kind of reformatting: We must process the world—and our place in it—differently.

In this chapter we'll look at yet another model of the process of grieving. This one takes a decidedly active approach and a clearly outward focus. Grieving is not just about learning to accept loss, but about re-engaging with the society around us. And perhaps our experience of pain and sorrow will actually prepare us to live more effectively in a challenging world.

THE TASKS OF GRIEF

In the last decade or two, some counselors have grown dissatisfied with the classic "stages of grief" model. In a sense, there was something too geographical about it. "You are here (at this stage) now. You'll be here for a while, and there's nothing you can do about it. When the time is right, you'll be over *there*." Wasn't there something more proactive that people could do to work through their grief? Was it really just a matter of waiting out their feelings, like a hockey player's trip to the penalty box or a young child's "time out"?

Only people who are capable of loving strongly can also suffer great sorrow, but this same necessity of loving serves to counteract their grief and heals them.

Leo Tolstoy

While the classic stages are still used (and, as we saw in chapter 3, sometimes added to), and other counselors prefer to speak of the "phases" of grief, there's increased talk about the "tasks" of the grieving process. In his book *Grief Counseling and Grief Therapy,* psychologist William Worden writes about a theory he calls "The Four Tasks of Mourning." This has widely caught on among counselors who recognize that it brings a more energetic sense to grief therapy.

"The tasks approach gives the mourner some sense of leverage and hope that there is something that he or she can actively do," writes Worden, "...although this may seem overwhelming to the person in the throes of acute grief, it can, with the facilitation of a counselor, offer hope that something can be done and that there is a way through it. This can be a powerful antidote to the feelings of helplessness that most mourners experience."

In this theory, you have several jobs to do as you recover. It's still a process, and it still takes time, but you are actively working through it. You are adapting and adjusting to a new kind of life without your departed companion. As with the stages of grief from the last chapter, there is a general order, but the tasks often overlap. "Tasks can be revisited and reworked over time," says Worden. "Various tasks can also be worked on at the same time. Grieving is a fluid process." According to Worden, there are four tasks of grief.

Task 1: Accept the reality of the loss.
This is the flip side of denial. Since denial is a normal first reaction in the grieving process, there's no shame in being there—

just as long as you don't stay there. Your task over the coming weeks and months is to accept the reality of your pet's death.

This is not just an intellectual acceptance, but an emotional one as well. You may know that your pet is gone, but still half-expect it to come bounding around the corner. There are many stories of pet owners who "forget" their pets are gone, and call out to them. If this has happened to you, don't feel bad. It doesn't mean you're crazy. It just means you still have a little work to do on this task.

Worden notes that acceptance needs to encompass the basic fact of the loss suffered, its meaning, and its irreversibility. When people deny the meaning of a loss, they may downplay the importance of the departed one. A pet owner says, "Well, it was only an animal. I didn't care that much anyway." While this may temporarily shield a person from the sorrow of losing a beloved pet, it's still a form of denial. The acceptance required in this first task means owning up to the importance of the pet in your life. It means fully facing your loss.

What can you do to help accomplish this task?

● **Have a memorial service.** In general, rituals move us through the transitions of life. It might help you deal with this transition if you set up a little gathering for family and friends who knew the departed pet. You don't need to make it a big production; just take the opportunity to express your appreciation for your pet and ask your friends for support as you grieve. This is especially helpful if you were not present at your pet's actual death, if you haven't seen the body, or if the pet has run away and is presumed dead. A service can provide much-needed closure.

● **Set a date to let go of your pet's things.** You may want to keep your pet's things—leash, bowls, cage, or what have you—around for a few days or even weeks, but don't keep them much longer than that. Put a date on your calendar to get rid of the items and stick with it. It will be an emotional time for you, so you might ask a friend to help.

● **Don't overreact to slip-ups.** So you forget and put out a bowl of food for your pet. Don't make a big deal of it. It's just your heart's way of saying a long goodbye to a cherished friend. This isn't a race; don't put too much pressure on yourself to hustle through your grief. Healing takes time.

Task 2: Experience the pain of grief.

This might be harder than you think. Society tends to frown on outward displays of emotion. Break down in tears and people might look oddly in your direction, as if you're not "normal"— which is ironic, because it's really the holding back of emotion that's abnormal. We were made to express our feelings, and we are healthier when we do so.

You may feel a certain pressure to be further along in your recovery than you are, so you'll stifle your tears or angry outbursts. You want people to think you're doing just fine. This too is ironic, because your effort to appear healthy is actually hurting your health.

Perhaps you're afraid to give in to your emotions because they might pull you down into a pit of depression. As a result, you hold back your true feelings, you just don't "go there." If this is the case, you might have a backlog of unspent emotion, perhaps from previous losses that were never adequately mourned. If so, you may want to talk with a professional counselor. He or she can help you unpack those emotions and dismantle those emotional blocks. (And don't worry that a counselor will laugh at you for grieving over a "mere" pet. If they have any training at all, they'll know how difficult this can be.)

Perhaps you find it uncomfortable to experience your grief because you don't know how. You would classify yourself as an "unemotional" person. Tears don't come easily to you. And maybe that's true. Or maybe you've become such an expert at holding back your feelings that it's now second nature to you. Don't force it. After all, no one benefits from a phony display of emotion. But

---

Ups and Downs

"Don't be surprised if just when you thought you were feeling better, you feel yourself crash again. This is normal," says psychologist Linda R. Harper, facilitator of the WINGS Pet Loss Support Group. Any little memory of your pet may get you crying again. Even simply seeing another animal similar to your pet on TV could lead you to dwell on your own loss. This is not a setback in your recovery. It just means that your feelings are still fresh, and you have a few tears left to shed.

you might want to start talking more about what you feel, whatever you feel. Talk with trusted friends, talk with yourself, talk with God—as an exercise, you may even talk with your departed pet. Let the walls fall down as you discuss how you really feel.

The only way through this grief is *through* it. Stop avoiding it, hiding it, or barricading it. Feel it. Yes, it will hurt. A lot. But that's the only way to accomplish this task.

What can you do to help accomplish this task?

● **Talk about your feelings.** Look for friends who will let you sob in their presence. Right now, you need listeners who won't try to cheer you up or calm you down, but will let you feel the way you really feel. If you don't have someone like that in your life, then look to a counselor or minister.

● **Join a pet bereavement group.** If not in person, you can find chat rooms online in which you can share and read others' experiences. Run a search for "pet loss" and try some of the sites that pop up.

● **Express yourself in the arts.** If talking isn't your thing, try writing about your feelings. Or painting. Or sculpting. Or making music. You don't need to create a masterpiece for public consumption; just let your emotions spill out. Work with the assumption that no one else will ever see this—and then take a chance with what you create. Dig up those feelings you have a hard time discussing.

● **Get physical.** Exercise is good for you, of course, and it's easy to overlook it in a time of grief. But if you have a swarm

of feelings buzzing within you, a good workout will get that
energy out. Walk, run, swim, lift, spin, or hit a punching bag,
and let your motion be powered by emotion.

● **"Steer into the skid."** If you've ever driven in an icy climate,
you might have heard the advice "steer into a skid." It sounds
counterintuitive. If your car starts to slide one way, you want to
steer yourself out of it, don't you? Nope. That would make you
lose control; the car would spin. Steering *into* a skid allows you
to regain control of the vehicle and drive safely out of danger.

Emotionally, you might find yourself "skidding." You're getting
into frightening territory, feeling shades of grief you're not sure
you can handle. Your instinct is to protect yourself from pain
or embarrassment by shutting down the feelings. But think of
that sliding car. Allow yourself to steer into that emotion, at
least a little.

Task 3: Adjust to an environment in which the deceased is missing.

Worden discusses three types of adjustments that are necessary in
dealing with grief: external, internal, and spiritual.

External adjustments have to do with the functions of everyday
life. If in the past your dog always fetched your slippers, you'll
need to get them yourself. One of the immediate challenges for
many pet mourners is the change in schedule. For example, if
your pet had a certain feeding time, walking time, or perhaps
playing time, it might take some time to get used to life without
those activities or timetables.

Internal adjustments have to do with your sense of self. This may or may not come into play for a pet owner. Without her cat, a woman who describes herself as the "crazy cat lady" might have to rethink that description. A man who shows up in the park as "Rover's owner" will need to find another way to introduce himself. If there were any guilt issues involved in the pet's death, this too might require some internal adjustments. For instance, a person who chose not to go forward with a pet's surgery or who put their pet to sleep might wrestle with guilt. But that person could also put a positive spin on the situation: "I am a person capable of making life-or-death decisions." We learn about ourselves in trying times.

Spiritual adjustments have to do with religion, fate, and the world. The death of someone close to us—whether human or animal— challenges the basic assumption many people have: that the world is fair and friendly. We may go through life expecting that good things will happen to us because we're good people, and then we suffer the sudden illness and death of a pet we love. *Why did this happen? Didn't we deserve better? Didn't our innocent pet deserve better?* Now the world doesn't make as much sense; it seems cruel and dangerous. It's a crisis of belief in ourselves, God, or the world around us that may require a major adjustment.

For many children, adjustments like these are a memorable part of the growing-up process. Years later, you'll hear people saying, "I learned as a child that the world is a nasty place," or, "I didn't want to believe in a god who would do that to my dog," or, "I figured I must have done something very bad to have my pet taken away like that."

This task requires a certain ability to "roll with the punches." We must accept that the world looks different after this tragedy, and that we must change with it. We struggle to make sense of things, but the breakthrough might come in finally accepting that life *doesn't* always make sense. Questions go unanswered. The world is not a neat equation. After your loss, you may be faced with this realization.

Grief at a Glance

Stages of Grief	Tasks of Mourning
Kübler-Ross, et al	*Worden*
Denial	Accept reality
–Pain/Guilt	Experience the pain
Anger	Adjust to new environment
Bargaining	Relocate the deceased/ Move on
Depression	
–Testing/ Reconstruction	
Acceptance	

What can you do to help accomplish this task?

● **Change your routine.** This is a simple adjustment you can make. Go out for a walk, but at a different time than when you used to walk the dog, and take another route. Routines you had established with your pet should be changed a bit, so that you can move on. (Of course, this isn't such a good idea if you still have other pets that depend on that routine.)

● **Be careful with medication of all types.** Adjusting is hard work, and you might be tempted to escape into alcohol, illegal drugs, or even misuse of prescription drugs. But try to abstain—you'll need to stay sober to take these important emotional steps.

● **Call for reinforcements.** Talk with the people who know you best. Ask them what they like best about you. That might seem odd to fish for compliments, but think about it this way: For some time now, you've enjoyed the unconditional love of a pet who thought you were divine. Now you need to get that support from people.

● **Find a new adventure.** Learn more about yourself. What makes you *you?* What skills do you have? What interests? What's on your "bucket list" of things to do someday? Now's the time to start cultivating those things! Learn a language. Start a new hobby. Travel. Maybe it was difficult to travel when you had a pet to care for, but now you're building a new life independent of the one you've lost.

● **Get spiritual counsel.** If you're nursing a grudge against God/ fate/the world, talk it over with someone who won't scold you. (Some clergy are good about this; some aren't.) Look for the most spiritual people you know (not necessarily the most religious), and have a chat with one of them. Talk a little and if they're open to it, talk more. See what wisdom they have to share.

Task 4: "Emotionally" relocate the deceased and move on with life.

What does it mean to "relocate" your departed pet? We're talking about your heart and mind here; where do you hold their memories?

Psychologist and writer William Worden called this task to "withdraw emotional energy and reinvest it." That may sound sort of clinical or confusing, but the idea is that it's time to stop investing your emotional resources in the one who's gone and time to start investing in your future. Worden got this idea from Sigmund Freud, who wrote, "Mourning has a quite precise psychical task to perform: its function is to detach the survivors' hopes and memories from the dead."

But it's not really a matter of "detaching." You don't remove the departed one from your heart—you can't. But you can "relocate" the deceased. You can put them in a place where you can always think of them fondly, but without being distracted by those memories. You're able to focus on building a new life. It's like taking a video screen off the dashboard of your car and putting it in the back seat. You still know it's there, and maybe you'll pull over sometime and watch what's on the screen. But if you want to get anywhere, it can't be right in front of you. Relocation is crucial.

This sounds easier than it is. Many people are afraid that if they take their memories of the deceased off the "dashboard" of their lives, so to speak, they'll forget them entirely. They feel it would somehow dishonor the departed to stop thinking about them. But nothing could be further from the truth, especially in the case of a departed pet.

Think about it. Your pet loved you. Your pet was fully invested in helping you live your life. Okay, it liked food and exercise and maybe a scratch behind the ears, too, but apart from that, it wanted what was best for you. Your pet was there for you in the midst of some difficult times. Well, this is a difficult time, and you're at a point where you need to move forward, not backward. You need to put memories of your pet in their place and focus on what's ahead. That's what's best for you now. And really, your pet would be more than willing to jump in the back seat and let you drive.

What can you do to help accomplish this task?

● **Create a memorial.** Find a fitting way to honor your departed pet—create a photo collage, name a small part of your home after your pet ("Champ's Corner"), or use a favorite pet toy to decorate the garden. Don't make this memorial an all-consuming passion; the idea is to show your love for your pet in a small way. (See Chapter 7 for more memorial ideas.)

● **Write a brief history of your life with your pet.** This is another kind of memorial. Don't worry about grammar or spelling. This probably won't be for public consumption, but it could be your personal tribute. It will be especially effective if you conclude with a section like "What my pet taught me," or "How my pet prepared me for the future." This is part of "relocating"—honoring the pet in the past, while you focus on moving forward.

- **Work on your human relationships.** It's possible that in your time of grief you've let your human relationships slide a little. This is the time to take stock with the handful of people closest to you. Do you need to reconnect with them, patch things up, or start anew?

- **Rediscover your creative, adventurous, fun side.** You've been through the wringer emotionally. You've had your time to mourn, but now it's time to dance—or it will be soon. Plan some fun experiences for the near future. Start enjoyable projects. Hang out with people who delight you. You've been distancing yourself from the joy of life; soon you'll be ready to move into really living again.

- **Give of yourself.** Here's a secret: Pain and loss equip you to help others. You have now "been there," and that enables you to commiserate with anyone else who is going through a rough patch. One of the surest ways to climb out of your pain is to care about someone else's. Try volunteering as a tutor, mentor, or helper for some nonprofit organization. Or connect with a community group or place of worship. Stay on the lookout for people experiencing grief, because you now have the qualifications to help.

Should You Get Another Pet?

Early in the recovery process you might be tempted to "replace" your departed pet with a new one, perhaps even one of the same breed and color. However, this is a classic example of bargaining, where you hope a quick fix will cure your grief. It may take a while before you're emotionally ready to open your heart to a new pet. In addition, it's not fair to expect a new pet to take the departed one's place, as if it were simply a replica. Wait until you're ready to love a new pet for his or her own personality.

It's possible that a well-meaning friend or relative will buy you a new pet to replace the old one. This also is not a good idea—only *you* know when you're ready to take on a new pet. Let them know you appreciate the gesture, but you're not quite there yet.

Sometimes children will beg and plead for a new pet, to replace the old one. It's advisable to hold off for now, at least during the early stages of grief. Instead, teach your children the importance of honoring their departed pet. Help them deal with the loss in a healthy way first, before getting a new pet.

Eventually, getting a new pet could be a good step forward. It will require you to open up your heart again. When you think you might be ready, visit an animal shelter—but at first you should only look around, not adopt. If you're feeling positive after the shelter visit, and you're still feeling good after you've thought about it for a few days, then maybe you're ready to make another commitment to a new animal friend.

Chapter 5

Will I See My Pet in Heaven?

*If having a soul means being able to feel love
and loyalty and gratitude, then animals
are better off than a lot of humans.
You've nothing to worry about there.*

JAMES HERRIOT

On one day each October, some unusual parishioners attend the Cathedral of St. John the Divine on New York's Upper West Side. The beautiful house of worship is filled with thousands of cats, dogs, rabbits, hamsters, monkeys, lizards, birds, and even the occasional llama. On this day, the church celebrates the life of St. Francis of Assisi, well known for his kindness to all creatures, by holding an annual Blessing of the Animals. Worshippers begin to line up early in the morning with their beloved pets in tow.

Is this just a gimmick to build attendance? Hardly. This church is renowned for its commitment to all of creation. Why shouldn't they ask the Creator's blessing on the animals that hold such a special place in people's lives?

"The idea of blessing is a little mysterious," says Reverend Linda Richardson, deacon of the Church of the Savior in West Chicago, which also has an annual Blessing of the Animals. "When we bless a person or a pet, we're extending God's favor. We're saying that this life is worth something. When we bless a pet, we're also blessing the owner and the relationship between owner and pet."

DOGS AND DOGMA

But what kind of relationship does God have with our pets? Do pets have any awareness of God? The intersection of faith and animals has long been a matter of wonder, conjecture, and debate. Theologians of various religions have commented on it, and some thoughtful prose and poetry have been written on the topic.

These questions become even more important to us when a pet dies. Suddenly it's not an abstract discussion anymore. It has personal emotional impact. When a human loved one passes away, we console ourselves with the idea that we will reconnect with him or her in the afterlife. When we lose a pet that we have loved, can we say the same thing? Will we be reunited with our pets in heaven?

The answers will most likely depend on your particular religious persuasion. This book cannot give you definitive answers to these questions. Consult your clergy or spiritual advisors, but don't be surprised if in the end they say, "We really don't know." Questions about our pets usually end up scampering past pure theology. However, many pet owners have deep feelings about these issues, and so they *sense* that there's a certain connection with their animals that will last for eternity. With that said, let's dig into these questions and see what we can learn.

When we're looking at the eternal destiny of our pets, it seems that there are three main questions involved.

Do animals have souls? (Particularly, does my pet have one?)
How do you define *soul*? Some might call it "personhood" or "spiritual value." For the purposes of this question, let's say it's "the ability to relate to the Creator." Can an animal "know" God in some way? Can an animal make a moral choice? In some religions, it is precisely the soul that distinguishes humans from animals. Others would hold that all beings have the ability to connect with the divine.

Are there animals in heaven? This depends on how you picture heaven (or whatever afterlife your religion believes in). Various pieces of religious literature give us glimpses of what heaven might entail. In some of these, animals are present; in others they're not. And there are some religions that don't believe in a heaven at all.

> *If I have any beliefs about immortality, it is that certain dogs I have known will go to heaven, and very, very few persons.*
>
> James Thurber

Will I have the same connection with my pet in that existence? This is the most important question for the grieving pet owner. If there are animals in heaven, and if my pet makes it there, will we recognize each other when I get there? Will the same love exist between us? Again, there are different ideas of what heaven will be like. Some people say all the good things of earthly life—including the love of a pet—will be present in heaven, while others say it will be an entirely different kind of existence.

A SURVEY OF RELIGION

Let's take a look at some of the prominent religious traditions in our culture and see how they address the question. But remember: We are summarizing and generalizing different religious views. You can investigate in more detail for yourself.

Islam sees God as judge of all, both humans and animals, which suggests that animals might have something akin to a moral soul. Paradise is seen as a place of pure delight, where people receive everything they ask for. Presumably, a pet owner who asked for their pet would not be denied. While there is no explicit teaching on the matter, there are these positive inferences.

Buddhism has no definitive answer about pets in heaven either. The idea of a future "heaven," whether for humans or animals, is not important to some Buddhists. The emphasis is on the present moment. All life is interconnected, and pets are honored as our fellow beings and as part of the richness of life, though they occupy a lower realm of existence.

In **Hinduism**, the divine is within every being, and so pets should be honored as manifestations of the divine, though their souls are of a lower form than humans. Their souls are reincarnated, and may eventually reach the human plane, which can then find oneness with the divine. (In one of the epic stories found in the *Mahabharata,* a hero insists on taking his pet dog on a chariot to heaven. Initially this is not allowed, but the hero maintains that the dog is a manifestation of a god. The dog turns into that god, and the hero is rewarded for his faithfulness.)

Mormons believe that animals have spirits and that they will go to heaven. According to the *Sacred Truths of the Doctrine and Covenants,* "They will be resurrected and placed in their appropriate places in Heaven. As the fall of Adam affected animals, so also through the atonement will the animals be heirs of salvation in their respective spheres." Elsewhere it says, "In the eternities the animals and all living creatures shall be given knowledge, and enjoy happiness.... These creatures will not then be the dumb creatures that we suppose them to be while in this mortal life."

Judaism has no official position on the matter. Many Western Jews are taught that there is no heaven or afterlife, but that people live on through others and through their good deeds. However,

If there is a heaven, it's certain our animals are to be there. Their lives become so interwoven with our own, it would take more than an archangel to detangle them.

Pam Brown

some traditional Jewish sources also teach that animals do have souls. Whether a pet's soul is reunited with its owner's is still debated.

Catholicism officially holds that pets do not go to heaven. Even so, the great medieval scholar Thomas Aquinas theorized that animals do have souls, but of a different sort than humans have.

Protestants have a wide range of beliefs on many matters, including this one. A number of Protestant leaders and scholars through the centuries have weighed in on the matter. Some are so focused on getting people to heaven that they're afraid the pet question is a distraction. Others see strong evidence in the Bible that animals will be in heaven.

WHAT THE BIBLE SAYS

Since there are so many questions about the Bible's teaching on this matter, we'll explore these documents further. As you may know, the Bible is a collection of Jewish and Christian writings from different times and situations. It's not a textbook that gives definitive answers to all of our questions, but it provides a host of helpful ideas and images about animals and heaven.

The Beginning

The Bible's opening chapters describe the creation of Earth and its residents. The creation is presented progressively, with each new "day" of creation seeing a new level—from heavenly bodies to plants, to animals, and eventually to humans. Animals and humans were both created on the sixth day. After each day, God looked at his handiwork and "it was good." After the creation of humanity, we're again told, "it was very good" (Genesis 1:31). The humans are given dominion "over every living thing that moves on the earth" (Genesis 1:28). Already there's a distinction between humans and animals.

Chapter 2 seems to retell the story of creation, this time with close-ups. God fashioned the first human from the dust of the earth, "and breathed into his nostrils the breath of life, and the man became a living being" (Genesis 2:7). The Hebrew word for "living being," *nephesh*, is sometimes translated as "soul." Many scholars would say that this was the point when humans were separated from animals. Thus, humans had souls; animals didn't.

Further, we see the man exercising his God-given dominion by naming the animals. But in the next chapter we find the first human sin. You may know the account of the forbidden fruit in the Garden of Eden. As a result of their disobedience, Adam and Eve were banished from the beautiful garden. At that point, the whole of creation suffered because of the Fall.

Life is eternal and love is immortal;
And death is only a horizon,
And a horizon is nothing save the limit of our sight.
Rossiter W. Raymond

From this story, some have suggested that domesticity is the natural way for animals to live. We generally assume that the natural life of animals is in the wild, but some biblical scholars say God's original intention was for humans to have dominion and responsibility over animals—much like your relationship with your pet. The wildness of the animal kingdom, they say, is a result of the Fall.

Ongoing interactions

We find animals entering the Bible's story at many points along the way, sometimes in surprising manners. This gives us important clues as to how God feels about animals.

● **Noah's ark.** When God destroyed the world by flood, he had Noah rescue animals, two by two. When it was over, God promised he would never again flood the earth, and he sent a rainbow as the sign of this promise. He told Noah, "I am establishing my covenant with you and your descendants after you, *and with every living creature that is with you, the birds, the domestic animals, and every animal of the earth with you, as many as came out of the ark*" (Genesis 9:9–10, emphasis added).

● **The Sabbath.** In one of the two listings of the Ten Commandments, God establishes a day of rest not only for people but also for "your ox or your donkey, or any of your livestock" (Deuteronomy 5:14).

● **Sheep and sparrows.** "The Lord is my shepherd," says the best-known Psalm (23:1), and later Jesus calls himself "the good shepherd" (John 10:11). This gives us a beautiful image of God's care for us, and implies that he also cares for animals. Jesus said directly, "Are not five sparrows sold for two pennies? Yet not one of them is forgotten in God's sight" (Luke 12:6).

- **God's helpers.** In some oddball stories, God used animals to do his work. The prophet Balaam was riding his donkey when the animal stopped along the path. Balaam grew upset at the donkey (although the beast brayed right back at him!), but he didn't realize the delay was because the donkey had seen an angel along their path—one whom Balaam couldn't see.

The wolf shall live with the lamb,
the leopard shall lie down with the kid,
the calf and the lion and the fatling together,
and a little child shall lead them.
The cow and the bear shall graze,
their young shall lie down together;
and the lion shall eat straw like the ox.
The nursing child shall play over
the hole of the asp,
and the weaned child shall put its hand
on the adder's den.
They will not hurt or destroy
on all my holy mountain;
for the earth will be full of the
knowledge of the Lord
as the waters cover the sea.

Isaiah 11:6–9

(Numbers 22). In another story, during a famine, God used ravens to feed the prophet Elijah (1 Kings 17:6). And of course in one well-known tale, the prophet Jonah was swallowed and redirected by a large fish, or whale (Jonah 1:17). Whatever else these stories teach us, they indicate that animals can serve God as humans do, and sometimes even better than the humans.

Future redemption

In both the Hebrew Scriptures and the Christian New Testament, prophets imagine a future world of peace, where all creatures will live in harmony.

● The book of Isaiah includes messages to people in critical times spanning a couple of centuries. They all needed a glimpse of hope, and they got it. Isaiah shows a scene where "the wolf will live with the lamb" (11:6), and a later prophecy declares, "the lion shall eat straw like the ox" (65:25). This is all part of the "new heavens and a new earth" that God will create (65:17).

● The New Testament book of Revelation is full of rich images, including "beasts" (or "living creatures") that worship God (Chapter 5). The Savior is depicted riding a white horse (19:11). Throughout the book he is identified as a Lamb. In this vision, John saw that is rife with symbolic picture-language, but it's still interesting that animals are featured so prominently.

● A crucial passage in this discussion is Romans 8:18–23, where the Apostle Paul takes a very wide view of Earth's history. The whole of creation, he says, has been "groaning," waiting "with eager longing" for God's final redemption of humans. The hope is that "the creation itself will be set free from its bondage to decay."

Flash back to the Garden of Eden, the original sin, and the curse. In Christian theology, that's when pain, death, and decay entered the world. All creation—humans, animals, and presumably even the plants and tectonic plates—shared the effects of that curse. Paul is saying that all creation will share in the glory of final redemption.

EXPERT OPINION

A little girl once asked Martin Luther, the renowned 16th-century Reformer, whether her recently deceased little dog would be in heaven. While acknowledging that we don't know everything about that future world, Luther responded, "All creatures will not only be harmless but lovely and joyful, so that we might play with them . . . Why, then, should there not be little dogs in the new earth, whose skin might be as fair as gold, and their hair as bright as precious stones?"

John Calvin, another 16th-century Reformer and a founding theologian of the movement that spawned the Reformed and Presbyterian churches, was a bit more cautious. He wrote that all creatures, "according to their nature, shall be participators of a better condition; for God will restore to a perfect state the world, now fallen, together with mankind. But what that perfection will be, as to beasts as well as plants and metals, it is not meet nor right in us to inquire more curiously." He noted that some were inquiring about the immortality of certain animals, and he worried about where such "speculations" would lead.

John Wesley, 18th-century preacher and founder of the Methodist Church, also had a fascinating description of the future, heavenly life of animals:

Your righteousness is like the mighty mountains, your judgments are like the great deep; you save humans and animals alike, O Lord.

Psalm 36:6

"The whole brute creation [that is, all animals] will then, undoubtedly, be restored, not only to the vigor, strength, and swiftness which they had at their creation, but to a far higher degree of each than they ever enjoyed. They will be restored, not only to that measure of understanding which they had in paradise, but to a degree of it as much higher than that, as the understanding of an elephant is beyond that of a worm. And whatever affections they had in the garden of God, will be restored with vast increase; being exalted and refined in a manner which we ourselves are not now able to comprehend. The liberty they then had will be completely restored, and they will be free in all their motions. They will be delivered from all irregular appetites, from all unruly passions, from every disposition that is either evil in itself, or has any tendency to evil."

Wesley saw the "horridness" of the appearance of some animals "exchanged for their primeval beauty. And with their beauty their happiness will return." What's more, God would pay them back for the suffering they endured on earth. While Wesley stopped short of saying that God treated humans and animals equally, he affirmed, "the Father of All has a tender regard for even his lowest creatures."

Twentieth-century British writer C. S. Lewis was perhaps best known for his series of children's books, *The Chronicles of Narnia.* He also was quite a philosopher. In *The Problem of Pain*, he put forth a unique theory: Not all animals will be in heaven—only those that are pets of people who are going to heaven. An animal, he suggested, "acquires its selfhood" by being in a relationship with a master or family. "And in this way it seems to me possible

What lovelier feature in the newness of the new earth, than the old animals glorified with us, in their home with us—our common home, the house of our Father—each kind an unfailing pleasure to the other! Ah, what horses! Ah, what dogs! Ah, what wild beasts, and what birds in the air! The whole redeemed creation goes to make up St. Paul's heaven.

George MacDonald

that certain animals may have an immortality, not in themselves, but in the immortality of their masters."

PERSONAL BELIEF

You may or may not care what famous theologians say about pets in heaven, or how different churches interpret the Bible, or what various religions say about the afterlife. This is an intensely personal question, not just a matter for scholars to wrangle over. *Will I see my pet in heaven?* Many people have a gut instinct that the answer is "yes." Veterinarian James Herriot, author of *All Creatures Great and Small*, once fielded this same question. "I do believe it," he said. "With all my heart I believe it."

Author Ptolemy Tompkins, author of *The Divine Life of Animals*, says, "It's unsophisticated to think an animal is solely a machine and not a spiritual being." He's countering the opposite assumption, that only a mechanistic view is "sophisticated." Borrowing from many different world cultures throughout time, as well as modern accounts, his book traces the history of the belief that animals have souls.

Some folks who come back from the brink of death report near-death experiences in which they saw their old pets in "heaven." Now, the jury's still out on whether these people are actually taking jaunts to heaven or their brains are just calling up random memories, but many people take this as solid evidence that their pets will be waiting for them when they finally do pass away.

Author Helen Weaver discusses her relationship with her dog, Daisy, before and after its death in her book, *The Daisy Sutra:*

Conversations with My Dog. When Daisy became quite ill, Weaver engaged the services of "animal communicators," who claimed to channel the spirit of pets, before and after death. In multiple conversations with several different communicators, Weaver learned that Daisy's spirit was doing just fine, though her body was weak. The dog was feeling joy. Weaver noted that she wasn't sure whether the communicators were really channeling Daisy or not. "I don't know, and I don't think it matters," she says. "What matters to me is that the words carried a precise personality and a boundless love that I recognized as real."

Many people report to have felt the presence of their departed pets around them in the days and weeks after the pets died. Some claim to have seen or heard their pets in some ghostly manner. They take this as proof that pets have an eternal existence. Skeptics might say it's just the bereaved mind playing games, but it's hard to shake a person's firm conviction.

From small beginnings, they grow stronger and deeper as they run their course, and once they have begun they cannot be turned back: Thus it is with rivers, years, and friendships.

Ancient Sanskrit verse

For many, the case for the immortality of pets' souls comes down to the question of "Why not?" Essentially, they shift the burden of proof—who are we to say animals do not have souls? In doing this, we reason that we don't know for sure what's beyond the great chasm of death, so it makes as much sense to believe it's true as to believe it's not. That's what this reverse logic is suggesting: Perhaps we can't prove it's true, but can anyone prove it's false? And since we really *want* to believe it, then why not do just that?

Maybe that wouldn't stand up in a scientific debate, but that's where many bereaved pet owners end up. They can't imagine that God would keep their pets out of heaven, that the life force they've enjoyed so much in their pets would just end, not to mention the love they have received. As Wallace Sife concludes in his book, "Heaven is love, and pets always share that with us."

OVER THE RAINBOW

"The Rainbow Bridge" is a helpful story that gives comfort to many who have lost their pets. It's also a wildly popular Internet phenomenon.

What's especially fascinating about "The Rainbow Bridge" is that it has taken on a nearly religious devotion. The description of this heavenlike place where pets wait for us has met a deep need in many bereaved pet lovers. People don't just enjoy this prose-poem, they believe in it, and they find comfort in the ideas within.

The Rainbow Bridge

Just this side of heaven is a place called Rainbow Bridge.

When an animal dies that has been especially close to someone here, that pet goes to Rainbow Bridge. There are meadows and hills for all of our special friends so they can run and play together. There is plenty of food, water and sunshine, and our friends are warm and comfortable.

All the animals that had been ill and old are restored to health and vigor. Those who were hurt or maimed are made whole and strong again, just as we remember them in our dreams of days and times gone by. The animals are happy and content, except for one small thing; they each miss someone very special to them, who had to be left behind.

They all run and play together, but the day comes when one suddenly stops and looks into the distance. His bright eyes are intent. His eager body quivers. Suddenly he begins to run from the group, flying over the green grass, his legs carrying him faster and faster.

You have been spotted, and when you and your special friend finally meet, you cling together in joyous reunion, never to be parted again. The happy kisses rain upon your face; your hands again caress the beloved head, and you look once more into the trusting eyes of your pet, so long gone from your life but never absent from your heart.

Then you cross Rainbow Bridge together...

Chapter 6
Family Matters

—✳

We cannot tell the exact moment a friendship is formed;
as in filling a vessel drop by drop, there is at last a drop
which makes it run over; so in a series of kindnesses,
there is at last one that makes the heart run over.
JAMES BOSWELL

It was Christmas Day, and Brad and Rachel watched as their two sons ripped through the carefully wrapped packages. Jason, 11, and Sam, 9, were having a blast with their new toys and gadgets. Finally, someone said, "Where's Pookie?"

No one had seen the family cat all morning, which was unusual. Well, they figured, maybe it was spooked by all the early-morning merriment. They looked all through the house. They checked outside. They searched the neighborhood, calling out for Pookie.

What began as a festive day became increasingly frantic as Brad drove through the streets, hoping to catch a glimpse of the family's lost cat. Rachel went out to the backyard and prayed. The prayer was equal parts plea and complaint: *Help us find him!* and *Why did you let this happen today of all days?*

The boys went to bed that night terribly worried, and it was hard for them to get to sleep. "Maybe Pookie's just out exploring, and he'll come back tomorrow," said their parents. "That sort of thing happens all the time. We'll look again in the morning."

The next day, the family woke to a foot of snow on the ground, which hindered their search efforts. Their hearts ached as they imagined Pookie somewhere outside, cold and confused.

"Why would he run off like that?" the younger son, Sam, wondered.

"That's what cats do sometimes," said Rachel. "They're curious."

"Yeah," added his older brother. "Haven't you heard, 'Curiosity killed the cat'?"

They all knew *it*—death—was a distinct possibility, but they didn't want to think about it.

I love cats because I enjoy my home; and little by little, they become its visible soul.

Jean Cocteau

The next week brought a strange mixture of emotions for the whole family—sadness, but also a certain energy in trying to solve the mystery. Rachel figured that the cat must have scampered away when she took out the trash late on Christmas Eve. She knew it wasn't really her fault, but she still felt guilty. Meanwhile, the boys acted out a little. After a week, the family figured that Pookie was gone for good. Jason thought that the cat probably had been run over by a car. Sam disagreed; he was sure Pookie had joined the other cats behind the nearby supermarket and was probably having the time of his life.

Brad put the cat's favorite cardboard box in the backyard, along with a dish of water and some dry cat food. If Pookie did wander back, he'd be welcome, but the family was ready to assume the worst and move forward.

WHEN CHILDREN LOSE THE PETS THEY LOVE

Jason and Sam each had his own relationship with Pookie, and they dealt with the cat's disappearance differently. Each boy will have his own way of finding closure in the matter—coming to the realization that Pookie is gone for good—and each will have his own way of grieving.

Although the whole family has been shaken by this loss, Brad and Rachel have a responsibility as parents to shore up their family life, to manage the collective grief process, and to make sure their children have the resources they need for healthy mourning. It's a daunting task for any parent.

Children will grieve differently according to their ages, personalities, previous experiences, closeness to the pet, and circumstances of the pet's departure. There's no standard seven-step course that every family must go through. Your situation requires careful observation of your children, communication, patience, and wisdom. Along the way, you will find the "right answers" for your family, or at least discover some helpful ideas to get you through this difficult period.

For many children, the loss of a pet is their first experience with death. Younger children really don't know what death is; they have no category in which to place this event and so have no understanding of it. The pet is there, and then it's not, and everybody's sad. What's up? Somewhat older children may see death on TV and in video games but still be untouched by it personally. Others may not realize death's permanence.

All of this means that parents (or grandparents) may have to take on the role of teacher, instructing their children in this basic aspect of life—that is, death. It must be done carefully and sensitively, but also clearly.

For many children, this is also their first experience with grief. They are feeling emotions they've never felt before. Again, they lack descriptive language and the ability to identify and categorize their feelings. As adults, we are able to say, "Oh, I'm going through a bad time. I'm stressed. I'm grieving." But children don't know how to do that yet. They may find themselves angry or listless or restless, and they don't know why. They feel an ache in the pit of their stomach, or perhaps they begin thinking of their parents', or their own, mortality. Such complicated feelings are often new, and for the very young (toddlers), it may even be beyond their developmental abilities to effectively comprehend or cope with.

Parents should act as counselors and guides through this difficult time. They might need to demonstrate "good grief"—for example, by having a healthy cry or maybe forgiving some stressed-out behavior. By their own example, parents can teach children how to identify their feelings and express them in words, as language and comprehension go hand in hand. And children need regular reassurance that things will be better in the future, and that grief eventually gives way to normalcy.

These are teaching opportunities for some of the most important lessons of life. What children learn from this experience will help them to know themselves and to engage with the world in a healthy way.

> If a child has previously experienced the death of a beloved person, but has not fully dealt with it, the death of a pet can be doubly difficult, because it could trigger grief for the previous death as well. Be prepared to talk about both losses with your child.

"Children look for personal meaning in everything," write Michael Stern and Susan Cropper in *Loving and Losing a Pet*, "and when they struggle to deal with sad and previously unfamiliar events, they are in danger of reaching erroneous conclusions that open the door for self-blame, guilt, and misunderstanding, which in turn can have far-reaching implications for behavior and adjustment."

You may find that challenge a little bit intimidating. But why not turn that around to the positive? Yes, if you leave children to engage in this emotional struggle alone, without any guidance, negative emotional and psychological effects may occur later. But if you pay attention to your children, talk with them, and take the time to answer their questions and discuss their fears, you will be building a mature, well-adjusted person. And isn't that what parenting is all about?

AGE CONSIDERATIONS

It's not like clockwork, but children do go through certain developmental stages. Use this as a general guide to help your children deal with grief at their level.

0–2 years old

There's little to no understanding of death at this early age, but very young children will pick up on the emotions of people around them. If there's a lot of crying or tension in the air, these youngsters may feel anxious or worried. Reassure them with lots of hugs and calming words.

2–5 years old

At this age, children may not understand that death is permanent. Be direct about this. They may also worry that the pet is gone as a result of something they did. You may be tempted to shield children this young from the harsh reality of the situation, but they'll know something is going on, and their fears might be harsher than the reality. Be honest, but simple, in your explanations. Don't be surprised if those children exhibit regressive behavior—crying, thumb-sucking, or bed-wetting (that is, if they've already grown out of it). They are merely seeking pathways for their grief with a behavior that seemed to work for them or comfort them in the past.

5–9 years old

Children's minds are blossoming in this stage, and they're often very curious. They'll ask about (or imagine) the details of the pet's illness and death, and they may wonder about their own death or yours. This may border on "morbid fascination," but do your best to deal openly with the questions. Children sometimes bear some feelings of guilt and worry that they caused the pet's death in some way. They may also feel angry if they blame you or someone else for the death. If you euthanized the pet, you may need to review that decision with them step by step. This is also a time of "magical thinking" for children, in which they imagine a pet coming back or think that someone caused the death by wishing it. In this stage, grief often gets acted out socially in the form of rebellious behavior at school or violent actions with playmates. Give them healthier ways to channel these feelings—for example, by talking, writing, drawing, or playing sports.

10–12 years old
From this age on, children are mentally able to comprehend death, but they're probably inexperienced at dealing with it emotionally. They look to parents as models for processing their grief. They might feel denial, sadness, anger, bargaining, and depression but not necessarily understand those feelings. Give this child as much permission to experience these feelings as you give yourself—perhaps more. Be open and expressive about your own grieving process, and explain it as you go. "I know it's been a while, but I'm still sad about losing Butters. Maybe you are, too." Remember that your child's grieving process might be on a different timetable than your own. Don't rush kids through their feelings—just nudge them along.

13 and up
Everything from the previous age group applies here, with one big addition: the need for peer acceptance. Teenagers often live and die by their place in social groups, and so they're likely to let

those concerns affect the grieving process. With a handful of close friends, perhaps pet-owners themselves, who understand and support your teen, he or she should do just fine. But if the larger group mocks or scorns your child for mourning a "mere animal," your teen may squelch his or her natural feelings of grief. Feelings should never be buried when they can be healthfully expressed and released—to do so can have damaging consequences later in life.

An additional complication is the adolescent's need to find and express his or her own identity. You probably know already that the least effective way to get something done is to flat-out tell your teenager to do it. You'll find the same thing is true if you order them to let out their feelings.

The point is this: Your teen needs to find his or her own way to grieve. Keep checking in and continue communicating with your child. You can reveal your own grieving process, but let your teen find his or her unique pathway.

GENERAL GUIDELINES

Be honest and direct. Avoid the euphemisms for death we commonly use as adults, as children might not understand them. "Putting an animal to sleep" might seem like a fine way to gently break the news, but it might make a child worry at bedtime— *What if I don't wake up?* Don't say the animal ran away if it didn't. Don't blame it on the vet if he or she did nothing wrong. Don't say God took the pet to heaven because he loved it so much. Tell the truth.

There are multiple problems with these well-meant "white lies." Young children will extrapolate from what you tell them, and they'll misunderstand what's going on. If you need an operation and anesthesia "puts you to sleep," they might get frantic. Or perhaps they'll wonder what they did to scare the pet away forever. They might learn to distrust doctors, or even God. But they might also learn not to trust *you*, once they learn the truth. It's much better to establish open communication with children early on.

"At all ages, honesty is the best policy," says bereavement counselor Marty Tously. "That means using the words 'death' and 'dying,' and explaining the permanence of death. You do it gently but without confusing them as to what dying really means."

With that said, you should be sensitive to what children can take in at any particular stage of their lives. Be honest and direct, but don't give more information than they can handle. It's a good idea to ask them if they have any questions. And, since they might not know which questions to ask, it's even better to ask your children periodically to explain to you what happened. This will give you a glimpse of what they're thinking and an opportunity to fill in details or clear up any misconceptions.

Be authentic. You have your own grieving process to go through. If you stifle it for the sake of your kids, you hurt yourself emotionally, and you give your kids a bad model of mourning. Let the grieving happen, and talk about it openly with your children.

Talking is especially important. If you try to contain it, your grief can release in bouts of crying or displays of anger. Your kids will wonder if they're the ones making you sad or angry (and maybe they are, a little), so it's important to talk about it. "I was a little upset with you for not cleaning your room, but I yelled at you too much, and I'm sorry for that. I think it's because I still miss Mittens." That kind of communication will help them to deal with their own grief-based anger at some point.

> ## What if they ask...?
>
> After losing a beloved pet, children might ask all sorts of questions, and they might have others they're not asking. You might want to prepare for the following questions.
>
> *Why did the pet die?*
>
> *Where is the pet now?*
>
> *Is the pet with God?*
>
> *Will I ever see it again?*
>
> *Is the pet happy?*
>
> *Who takes care of our pet now?*
>
> *Can the pet see and hear us?*

There is one slight caveat to this guideline: As a parent, you're still in charge, and you're still responsible for the family. Especially in their time of grief, your children need to know that they're secure and that the family is operational. You need to let them know that you're not going to have a complete meltdown or leave them—both of which can be very scary to kids. So even if you're sad, angry, or depressed, you still need to cook dinner, drive them to school, and help them with homework, or at least see that those tasks get done. Don't burden the children with your woes or make

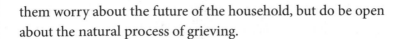

them worry about the future of the household, but do be open about the natural process of grieving.

Be there. Even if you have nothing to say, your presence is crucial in this time of need. Your child has suffered an important loss and may feel abandoned, rejected, or forsaken. You need to do all you can to counter those feelings. You don't need to have all the answers. You don't need to know all the right things to do. *Be there* and good things will happen as a result. Doing so puts you in a position to monitor your child's grief, and you can answer your child's questions as they arise.

As children get older and grow into the middle school and teen years, "being there" becomes more of a challenge. Your presence doesn't need to be as frequent, but it should be a priority. Children in this age group need time away from their parents for their own individuation, but awareness and communication within the family are still necessary. In a time of grief, some older children will want to spend less time at home, where they see constant reminders of the lost pet. Even so, being available is still extremely important, for them and for you. Studies have shown the strength of families that routinely have dinner together. Perhaps that's an option that will help your family to work in some "together time."

Be patient and permissive. Wait—permissive? Well, not in the sense that you let your children do whatever they want, but that you give them permission to grieve as they need to. You may encounter a frustrating time of denial when they talk about the pet coming back. As long as you've clearly explained the facts, you don't need to rush them out of denial. Don't try to keep kids from crying or asking questions. Even if *you've* had enough, realize that apparently they haven't. Be wise in the way that you deal with their anger. Understand that this is a way of coping with their loss, but you may also want to teach them about controlling their actions when they feel angry. This process may not develop the way you thought it would, and it may last longer than you want, but allow it to run its course. If you try to inhibit their emotions, the process may last even longer.

Be perceptive. Most likely you are already an expert on your children—after all, you've been reading their emotional and physical responses since birth. But in a time of grief, you need to be especially attuned to their reactions. They are navigating uncharted waters here, and they may not respond as you expect. "It is not uncommon for children to present a blank facade that can be interpreted as indifference or as no emotional reaction at all when anger or bitterness is clearly part of the experience," say authors Michael Stern and Susan Cropper. "Similarly, children may appear to return to a normal routine rather quickly, yet the loss continues to have its impact in subtle ways."

It's sometimes assumed that children aren't very serious about their grief when they move quickly from tears to laughter, but that's not necessarily the case. It can be their way of managing strange new emotions. In order to keep from being overwhelmed with sadness, they might "rescue" themselves with laughter.

All of this requires careful study and insightful perception on the part of parents. Stop, look, and listen to your children. Understand when they've received enough information for one day. Recognize when they have questions they don't know how to ask. Sense when they need a hug rather than an explanation. No one knows your children like you do, so trust your intuition, but keep studying and perceiving. What was true of them yesterday may not be true today.

Be a wise leader. As a parent, you steer this vessel we call a family. You make decisions that affect the whole family. So when the household is dealing with the loss of a pet, you have a certain responsibility to manage the recovery. You can't dictate how each family member will grieve, but you can take certain steps that might facilitate the process.

One important task is to set a tone of mutual support within the family. When there are multiple children in the household, some may appear to go through grief very quickly, while others carry the sadness for quite some time. You will need to foster an understanding among the family that grieving is an important task, and that each person has the right to do it in his or her own way.

You may have already made decisions regarding the death and burial or cremation of your pet. Perhaps you have also made decisions about whether to involve your family in those events. Doubts or concerns may be raised, even by you, but one role of a leader is to keep moving forward.

You might want to consider some sort of funeral or memorial for the lost pet in which the family can participate. Whether an event or an artwork or a monument, it might help your family to both honor the pet and gain a sense of closure so they can "let the pet go" and retain good memories. Lead the way forward—what do *you* think the family needs?

Also, be wise about whether and when to get a new pet. Your kids may want one right away, but this may not be a good idea. You need to gauge when they've sufficiently moved on so that a new pet is not just a quick stand-in for the old one but a unique being that can be loved in its own right.

In these and other matters, you need to manage not only your own grief but also that of your family. Gather information, process it, and make wise choices.

FAMILY CONFLICT

Oswald was an albino parakeet that stole Jeannie's heart. She bought the bird at a difficult time in her life, and it gave her joy when nothing else could. There was a cage upstairs in Jeannie's bedroom, but she let Oswald fly freely through the house.

Jeannie shared the house with her mother, who raised pug dogs. There were always several dogs in the house, and Jeannie's mother would take them to dog shows from time to time. Oswald got along great with the other pets. One of the dogs would let Oswald sit on her back and groom her. The bird took baths in the dog's water dish. Funnily, Oswald's favorite phrase was "I'm a lucky dog."

One day a terrible accident happened. Jeannie's mother was resting on the couch and suddenly rose to go into the kitchen. She accidentally stepped on Oswald as he was scuttling around the floor, fatally injuring the bird. Jeannie got home an hour or so later, but Oswald was barely alive. The vet said there was nothing to be done. Soon the joy-giving bird was gone.

You can imagine how horrible the mother felt. She apologized to her daughter profusely. Jeannie understood that it was an accident, and she didn't blame her mother, but she was deeply hurt by the loss of her avian companion. "Neither of us knew what to do with our grief," she now says, looking back. "It was just left hanging there."

The timing of this accident was especially unfortunate. Jeannie was to get married the following week. She was already in a flurry of activity, and the next week was even more frantic. With the marriage, the honeymoon, and moving into a new place with her husband, Jeannie never really had time to work through the issues of Oswald's death with her mother. There was a general haze of guilt, blame, regret, and sorrow, and they didn't talk about it. It remained there between them—never a matter of hate or anger, just distance. They didn't know what to say to one another.

When a pet dies, it may stir up tension within the family. The emotional turmoil during the aftermath may give rise to resentment and bitterness, guilt and blame, whether spoken or not. If these feelings are brought into the open, they can be discussed and dealt with, confessed, forgiven, and released. If not, the negative feelings can continue to fester, poisoning family relationships for years to come. Let's take a look at some of these adverse reactions.

Guilt can be a problem because it's not always rational. As we've seen, children can feel responsible for a pet's death (or disappearance) even if they had nothing to do with it. In the same way, adults can second-guess themselves for their decisions (such as putting a pet to sleep), even if those choices were legitimate. There's always another way to look at things—you may feel bad for putting a pet down too soon or too late, for involving the kids in the process or not, and even for the decision whether to cremate or bury. There is plenty of "phantom guilt" to be found in these matters.

It gets a bit more complicated when the guilt might actually be deserved. Maybe Pookie wouldn't have gotten out at night if Rachel had been more careful with the back door. Maybe. Perhaps you had a choice between paying for a pet's surgery and getting the new car you needed, and you chose the car. Maybe you left the dog in the car or the cat in the basement with unforeseen disastrous results. What can you do about those feelings of guilt?

Nancy fights back tears as she talks about an event that occurred several years earlier. She had two cats—an older, worldly outdoor cat and a younger one she had always kept inside. This double standard became hard to enforce, and so she began to let the younger cat outside during the day, trusting the older cat to teach it how to survive in the "wilderness" of her suburban community. One evening, Nancy called for the cats to come indoors. The older one came quickly, but the younger one didn't. As it turned out, it had been hit by a car and killed.

Nancy still feels guilt about the incident. The younger cat wasn't ready to be outside at night, she says. She should have called it in before dark. Her sense of regret runs deep.

A friend tried to console her. "You wanted to give that cat a certain kind of life where it could run and play freely outside. There's nothing wrong with that. Your cat would forgive you," he said.

That's really what guilt requires, isn't it? Forgiveness. The problem with guilt in a family situation is that it puts up walls. The guilty person withdraws from the others, whether or not they're being blamed. How do you break down those walls? By talking about the issue. Allow the guilty person to confess; let the others consider, and say, "We understand what you've done and we see your pain, and we will continue to love you. Let's put the matter aside."

Resentment is the flip side of that coin. This occurs when people blame others and hold grudges. "You never liked that cat anyway. You intentionally left the door open." This reasoning is often irrational and frequently unspoken. "I can't prove it, but I *know*."

Children sometimes feel resentment toward their parents if they're kept out of the euthanasia decision. All they know is that mom or dad took the pet to the vet and it didn't come back. Often children make the deduction that their parents must have killed it. Without knowing the whole story, it's easy for children to attribute negative motives. This can also happen with older children living away from home at college or elsewhere. If they suddenly hear that the pet was put to sleep, they might suspect that the parents were just tired of caring for *their* pet.

As we've seen, there are often financial decisions regarding the health of a pet, and they can also create resentment within the family. How important is the health of the pet compared to other pressing financial matters? Children often can't understand why healing a pet is less important than, say, paying the mortgage. Similarly, this can also be a source of tension between couples.

Joe had a three-year-old dog that broke its leg. The vet informed him that it would cost hundreds of dollars to set the leg. Joe decided that it was too costly, and so he had the dog put down. He had never really bonded with the dog anyway—but his wife had, and she was upset about his decision. She didn't want to have a big fight about it, so she never told Joe her feelings. But for years afterward, whenever she thought about that dog, she cried.

It's a mistake to think that issues like this will just go away over time. It's best to open up and talk about them. When all of the elements—blame and explanations, pain and confessions— are out in the open, it's easier for people to reconcile with one another and with the loss. Forgiveness becomes one of those elements.

Favoritism can spawn a certain kind of resentment that surfaces when a family loses a pet. Sometimes pets become associated with certain family members. It's "Maria's kitty" or "Johnny's dog," even if other family members love and care for the pet as well. When that pet passes, attention and sympathy may be showered on the one person associated with it, but not on others who also hurt. This can even be true of parents—often it's Mom or Dad who feeds the pet and provides most of the care. They can feel left out of the sympathy. It's important to see how *everyone* is struggling with the loss of the pet. Spread the sympathy around, and you'll avoid this type of resentment.

Wounds of the grieving process deserve mention as well. We've already seen how grief can lead to anger and depression. When one family member is experiencing these feelings, the rest of the family is affected as well. One sibling, hurt by the angry words of another, may respond in kind. A parent may resent the way a depressed teen "shut down" after a pet's death and now refuses to do anything around the house. Grief can sometimes blind people to the needs of others, and in a family in which everyone is suffering from the same loss, some people can feel neglected.

Once again, communication is key. If the family keeps sharing their feelings, they can help each other through the process and heal wounds incurred along the way.

Sorrow makes us all children again,
destroys all differences of intellect.
The wisest know nothing.

Ralph Waldo Emerson

SINGLES AND SENIORS

When we talk about "family matters," we sometimes overlook certain households; often these are the ones most deeply affected by the loss of a pet.

Single people, especially those who live alone, can find the grief devastating. A pet can do a great deal to keep loneliness at bay. It's something to talk to, something to care for, and something to cuddle with. A pet can bring a measure of wholeness to the lives of some singles. When that pet is gone, everything is shaken. The routines of life are thrown off. The owner has to deal not only with grief, but also loneliness and possibly a feeling of purposelessness. "For singles, the loss of a pet is like the loss of a child," says Thomas Whiteman, a psychologist who has written on the needs of divorced and single people. "That's their companion."

Further, the single person sometimes lacks a support network to provide comfort in this difficult time. The pet is the companion who was there for the owner in previous crises, and now the pet is gone. If you're a single person touched by the death of a beloved pet, what can you do? Here are some thoughts.

- **Don't take it lightly.** Your emotions are slamming you right now, and you may be uncomfortable with those feelings. *I shouldn't feel this bad. Does this mean I'm abnormal?* There is nothing abnormal about feeling thrown by the loss of a primary companion. You have nothing to apologize for.

- **Change your routine.** Presumably you did a number of things on a regular basis that involved your pet, whether it was walking the dog or watching your favorite TV show with your cat on your lap. These activities can remind you of your pet and drag you deeper into sadness. Find a different way to get exercise. Go to a friend's house to watch your show. Whenever possible, get out and engage with the world around you, rather than sit at home with your memories.

● **Write down your feelings.** You could also record your feelings or sing them or paint them—the point is to let them out. Many pet owners talk to their pets (and those pets are probably pretty good listeners!). Without that sounding board, it's easy to allow thoughts and feelings to stagnate within you. Let them out by journaling, composing, blogging, or by other means.

● **Find a support network.** Start with one friend who understands your pain—maybe it's a relative, a neighbor, or a coworker. If you're already connected to some sort of singles group, whether in a community or a church, look there for sympathetic friends. If not, consider joining one. (Just make sure the group is focused on friendship and not solely on matchmaking.) Groups are also available, online and in person, for those who have lost pets.

● **Watch out for a "rebound."** The grieving process makes you emotionally vulnerable. It's rather easy to get into an unhealthy romantic relationship when you are feeling needy. As with any new relationship, it's wise to go slowly.

● **Control your addictions.** This is another danger. When you're hurting, it's easy to seek relief or escape in alcohol, drugs, gambling, pornography, or even computer games. As a single person you have less accountability to others, especially if you live alone, so addictions are especially tempting.

- **Seek your purpose.** As you find yourself pulling out of the downward spiral of grief, it might be a good time to do some heavy thinking about your purpose in life. Is it rooted in your job, your hobby, your faith, or your friendships? Is there something you could be doing to pursue your purpose more directly?

- **Get another pet.** You'll know when you're ready. You already know that no other animal can replace the one you lost, but when the time is right, visit a shelter and make a home in your heart for another companion.

Senior citizens have many of the same issues as singles, even if they're married. Pets become part of the rhythm of their lives, and that comfortable routine is sorely missed when the pet is gone. In some cases, the pet has aged along with them, and they have a long history together. That makes the pain all the greater. It also brings an unwelcome reminder of their mortality. For widows and widowers, the pet might serve as a connection to the departed spouse, and so the grief doubles when the pet dies.

The social networks of seniors often shrink as they age, and now they find themselves without a good support system. It's difficult to get the comfort they need. For seniors that are married, the loss of the pet can leave both people emotionally needy. It helps to have a third party offer understanding and consolation.

If you're a senior citizen affected by the loss of a pet you loved, what can you do? First, read over the advice to singles, because many of the same ideas apply to you. In addition, consider the following ideas.

● **Memorialize the pet.** Make a scrapbook of pictures or craft some sort of shrine—not to worship the pet, but to honor its memory. Especially if the pet was with you for many years, you'll have a lot of memories, and you don't want to forget them.

● **Enjoy your freedom.** Were there activities, such as travel, that you couldn't do before, or were more difficult, because you had the pet? Exploring new adventures might be a good way to take your mind off your loss.

● **Consider the practical effects.** What did your pet do for you that is now missing in your life? Did it provide security in your home or on your walks? Did it help you get regular exercise? Did it remind you of certain things in your schedule? It wouldn't hurt to list these things and then think about how they will still be accomplished.

● **Talk about any guilt you feel.** If you're on a fixed income, perhaps you lacked the resources to pay for the pet's surgery. Or maybe it was too difficult to get the pet in for check-ups as often as you should have. Whatever the case, you might be feeling some guilt over your pet's death. The best way to deal with this is to talk it out, if not with your spouse, then with a friend or counselor.

- **Don't feel bad about crying.** This might not apply to you, but there are a number of older folks, especially men, who have learned not to show emotion. Some people may see tears as a sign of weakness. If that's your assumption as well, it may keep you from getting over your pet's death. So if you feel like crying, go ahead and cry. Tears are healthy when you are facing a serious loss. Holding them back is what hurts you.

- **Think through the issues of getting a new pet.** It may be a little more complicated for a senior citizen—considering income, living quarters, and the energy needed to care for an animal—but having a new pet can be very rewarding. Don't assume you can't get a pet at your age, but do look at all of the options first. For instance, you may want to share custody of a new pet with a younger person or family—a solution that would ease the burden on you and still provide some much-needed love and joy. If getting a baby animal such as a puppy or kitten seems daunting or just not right for you, consider adopting an adult pet. It's harder for shelters to find homes for grown pets, and getting an animal that's already housetrained can be a benefit to a senior.

- **Renew relationships.** Consider a renewed connection with children and grandchildren. You invested a lot of love in your pet, and now you don't know where to put that energy. Think about whether there are others in your life—humans or animals—who might benefit from your attention.

Chapter 7
Shaping Memories

—❋—

Until one has loved an animal,
a part of one's soul remains unawakened.
ANATOLE FRANCE

In Israel, about 30 miles south of Tel Aviv, archaeologists uncovered a burial ground for dogs that dates back 2,500 years. This find occurred at the ancient site of Ashkelon, not far from the Mediterranean coast.

"You run across buried animals all over the Middle East," said Lawrence Stager, a professor from Harvard University and the director of the dig, in an interview with *The New York Times*. "In Egypt, there are several pet cemeteries, where cats and other animals were mummified and buried. But this is not a pet cemetery. It is just for dogs, all the same breed, and a huge concentration of them. Nothing like it has ever been found before."

Several hundred graves were found, some with intact skeletons. According to the report, the remains were very similar, a breed resembling the greyhound, and each dog apparently "buried with great care, placed on its side in an individual grave, with its tail wound around its hindquarter and the tip pointing down."

The find has become an archaeological whodunit, or maybe a "whatisit," since the dogs appear to have died naturally. Was the site a sort of kennel or perhaps dog breeder's place? Was it a cult or the headquarters of the police K-9 unit of the time? We may never know. But what's striking about this story is the care with which these animals were buried. They weren't just put into the ground—these dogs clearly were honored. The fact that they were all laid out in the same way suggests there might have been a ritual involved, some sense of propriety. Did the people who performed the burial believe that these animals would enter an afterlife? (The Egyptians, not too far down the shoreline, held such beliefs.) Whatever the case, it seems that this culture cared about these animals, even in their death. They were concerned with how these animals would be remembered—and here we are, thousands of years later, "remembering" these creatures!

Ours is not the first culture to love pets, and it won't be the last. Throughout recorded history, humans and animals have forged strong bonds. This final chapter will address what to do with pets' bodies and give ideas for how can we most effectively honor their lives, remember what they've given us, and move on without our companions.

DEATH AT HOME

Whether expectedly or not, if your pet passes away at home, it can be difficult to know what to do with the body. You may be able to leave the body with a veterinarian, local shelter, or city sanitation department for disposal; call ahead and ask before making the trip. As the body will not maintain for long, the sooner this is handled, the better.

However, there are times when one must keep the body for a short period of time while a decision or arrangements are being made (or other circumstances). The American Society for the Prevention of Cruelty to Animals (ASPCA) recommends the following:

* Place the animal wrapped in plastic in a refrigerator or freezer. The exception to this is if you plan to have a necropsy performed to determine cause of death. Then the body should be refrigerated but not frozen. If you do want a necropsy performed, you must contact your vet as soon as possible after the death.

* If your pet cannot fit into a refrigerator or freezer, the body should be placed on a cement floor or concrete slab. Do not cover or wrap the body in this instance, as doing so will trap heat in the body.

* If neither of the above are options, then as a last resort you should keep the body (wrapped in plastic) in the coldest part of your home, out of the sun, and packed with bags of ice. The body will not decompose immediately, so there is no need to worry about odor.

BURIAL AND CREMATION

If your pet passes away at the animal clinic, you'll have to decide what to do with the body. Most veterinarians will dispose of the body if asked. Be sure to specify your wishes—it would be horrible to assume you had time to decide, but the doctor (unless he or she was told otherwise) went ahead and had the body cremated.

The main options for body disposal available to pet owners are burial and cremation. (Taxidermy and freeze-drying are also

Burying Your Pet at Home

In some states and cities, it's legal to bury an animal as long as you own the property. In others, there are regulations that forbid the burial of animals on private property. It's best to check with your local municipal office before proceeding. Here are some other things to consider.

● There may be municipal regulations about digging, for public safety and for fear that utility lines will be damaged. If you do not own the property or if you want to bury your pet on public property (like a favorite park), it will almost certainly be illegal.

● There may also be rules about how to bury your pet, particularly regarding the depth of the grave. Generally, it's a good idea to dig the grave two to three feet deep, so that other animals (or children) don't dig it up.

● In the past, it was suggested that the body be wrapped in plastic; nowadays biodegradable materials are preferred. Online vendors even sell eco-friendly pet caskets.

choices, but both have inherent difficulties, and we won't discuss them here). Factors such as cost and religious beliefs will come into play in your decision-making.

Your veterinarian should be able to help you make a decision. Even if you haven't euthanized your pet, the vet may be able to put you in touch with local pet cemeteries or give advice on burial options. Your local animal shelter or ASPCA chapter may also be of help. Don't be afraid to ask for advice or recommendations.

Pet Cemeteries

If you feel you need a location at which to remember your pet, then you might consider burial at a pet cemetery. These places offer beautiful surroundings where you can memorialize your pet with a gravestone or other display. However, such cemeteries can be costly. It will be up to you to determine whether you can afford the cost.

Home Burial

Many people choose a do-it-yourself approach with pet burial. If the pet is small, this can be done rather easily, but there are still questions to consider.

- Are there laws in your community regarding the digging of holes or the burial of animals?

- Is it important to you to have a nearby site (say, in the backyard) where you can remember your pet?

- What would happen if you move or if you build an addition or put in a pool?

- Would you put up any kind of marker?

- Would the burial occur as part of some sort of ceremony, giving friends and family a chance to say goodbye to the pet?

- Are you ready for the physical process of handling the pet's body in order to bury it?

Cremation

If your vet euthanized your pet, he or she will probably offer to have your pet's body cremated. Cremation is generally the easiest option, and it's often reasonably priced. If you choose this option, consider the following: Do you want your pet cremated by itself or with other animals? It's cheaper to cremate several animals at once, but if you want to keep the ashes (or "cremains") in an urn, jewelry, or some other container, your pet should be cremated alone.

> *In three words I can sum up everything I've learned about life: it goes on.*
> Robert Frost

Some people have strong feelings about the burning of a human body in cremation, but do the same feelings apply to a pet's body? Essentially, the difference between the methods has to do with the speed of destruction. Whether slowly by burial or suddenly by cremation, the body will be destroyed. But if you believe that the pet's essence lives on in spirit form, in memories, or in future resurrection, then the body has served its purpose and need not be preserved.

Because of public health concerns, scattering ashes is as legally tricky as home burial. It's best to check your state and local laws regarding the scattering of your pet's ashes.

MEMORIAL EVENTS

We humans mark out the major transitions of our lives with rituals: marriages, funerals, graduations, birthdays, baby showers, retirement dinners, and so on. These are gatherings that say, in essence, "That was then; this is now." A line is drawn. This couple walked into the room as separate people; they leave as one. This person was a student; now she's a graduate. When there's a big change in our lives, we often use ritual to show its importance.

If you have lost a pet, you are at a transition point. This creature was important in your life, and possibly that of your family. Now that pet will be important in your memory. Some people go further and feel a need to mark this event with a memorial service of some kind—a ritual, if you will, that honors their pet fittingly, and allows those who loved the pet to move on.

Keep in mind that it's not necessary to hold an event. Many people lose their pets and go on quietly without any official ceremony. But a memorial ceremony may help you find closure along your own grief journey. It can help you connect with supportive people. And it may honor your pet in a way that will close the book on its earthly life in an appropriate manner.

Planning the Event

Is it a little crazy to hold a funeral service for a pet? No, not at all. When we hold a funeral for a person, it's not really for him or her. It's a way for everyone else to say goodbye. A memorial service is not for the dead but for the living, and that holds true whether you're honoring a dearly departed human or animal.

The memorial may be connected to the final disposition of the pet's body, but it doesn't have to be. If you have chosen to bury the body, you may have a memorial event in addition to the burial. But even if there are no remains involved, you can still have a memorial to honor the pet's memory.

You might look into holding a service at a funeral home. Some morticians offer their facilities, normally reserved for humans, for pet funerals. They might be able to help you plan such a service as well. Again, these services will involve a fee.

But let's say you're having a simple memorial service in your own backyard. How will you do it? What's involved? Well, let's look at three ingredients involved in planning a memorial event.

Invite people who care. Your immediate family will likely be in attendance, but you may want to reach out to your friends as well, especially anyone who knew your pet—children who played with it, neighbors who watched your pet for you, and so on. You can always ask. Be gracious if they turn you down, but you may be surprised by who shows up.

Prepare to say a few words. You don't need to be a great orator; just speak from the heart. What did this pet mean to you? It might help to tell a fun story about the pet. You don't need to drag this out—just a few minutes is plenty of time. If you'd like, invite others to contribute with a favorite quote, poem, or a few simple words.

Make it artistic. Display a picture of your pet. Set up some of its favorite toys. You don't need balloons or streamers, but make your yard (or wherever) look a little different than usual. Are certain songs appropriate to the occasion? See what you can do to provide music for the event.

You might have two people at this memorial or you might have ten. It's not really important. Fight the urge to define "success" by

Liturgy for a Pet Funeral

Sometimes it's hard to find the right words to say. If that's the case for you, the liturgy below may be a useful model. Adapt it as you will. Feel free to make it more or less religious, and add appropriate songs, stories, or readings.

We're here this afternoon to commit_____ [the pet] to the Lord and to the earth. He/She has been a good pet for _____ [owner or family], who loved him and cared for him through-out his life.

The book of Proverbs says, "The righteous know the needs of their animals" (Proverbs 12:10), and this is true of you, _____ [owner or family]. You were tuned in to _____'s [pet's] needs and you provided for them.

It's always difficult to let a pet go, and we stand with you in this sorrowful time.

Let us all think of the beloved pets we have lost through the years. We live in the hope that we will see them again in heaven. There, our "mansions" will be full of God's little creatures.

We believe that you will see _____ [pet] there, too.

We look forward to a time when the Lord will set all things right and we will be reunited with all those we love. The pain and suffering of animals and humans will be no more. God will wipe the tears from our eyes.

God created the animals and he loves them all, and he loves you too, _____ [owner or family]. We pray you'll know his love in this time of sadness.

Thanks to Linda Richardson. Adapted and used by permission.

attendance numbers. What's important is that those who knew this animal best have the opportunity to share their appreciation and their love. When the pet is sufficiently honored, the pet-lovers can move on.

MEMENTOS

Terri was a single mom with two teenagers and a golden lab named Missy. The dog was seen as a caretaker and protector for the whole family and a source of strength and comfort through some difficult times. When Missy passed away, the family took it very hard, each member grieving in his or her own way. Terri wanted to make sure her kids had some mementos of Missy, so she found photos she had taken of each of them with the dog and made some copies. They each got a paw print from the vet. Terri also gave her son Missy's leash and her daughter the collar. At first, she wondered if those gifts would seem silly to teenagers, but they were in fact treasured.

Many of our best memories are associated with certain objects, and when we lose a pet, we can savor the memories by saving some mementos. It's not silly at all to distribute the toys or dishes of a departed pet. Some grieving owners put their pet's paw prints, photos, or ashes in key chains or pendants. They want to carry the memory with them. Photos are especially precious because they will help people visualize the pet even after the memories have long faded.

SPECIAL SITES

Is there a special place that your pet loved—a sunny spot by the window or perhaps a shelf in the laundry room? Another memorial idea is to make this place special by decorating it with pictures or mementos of your pet. Or use your gardening skills to plant a space in the garden that will remind you of the pet.

Darla was heartbroken when she had to put her 16-year-old Persian cat, Cookie, to sleep. Darla brought Cookie's body home from the clinic, wrapped the cat in a quilt, and buried her in a peaceful spot behind her house. "I planted a bag of pink tulips over her grave and tried to deal with the huge empty spot in my heart her passing had left."

Months later, Darla returned to the grave. "There was a feeling of spring in the air, so I went back to the site. It was covered with beautiful pink tulips! I have since moved from that house, but, 12 years later, every spring I think of Cookie and hope the tulips are still blooming."

CREATIVE TRIBUTES

As children deal with this sort of grief, it's often suggested that they draw pictures of the pet they've lost. Why shouldn't adults do the same thing? Perhaps the memory of your pet will inspire you to unleash your creative talents. Draw pictures. Don't just gather photos; put them in an album and decorate it appropriately. Make a scrapbook, including memories and stories by different family members. Write a poem. Keep a journal of your memories. Make a tribute video, interviewing everyone who knew the pet. Write a song. Make a mix CD or play list of songs that your pet would have loved (or did love) or tracks that remind you of your pet.

Of course, you may not be a professional artist. That doesn't matter. This creative output isn't about you becoming a star—it's about saying thanks to a pet that enriched your life. And it might also be an effective way to turn your mourning into dancing: Take the energy of your grief and transform it into creative expression.

MEMORIAL WEBSITES

You can post on various websites as a memorial for your pet. Simply do a search for "online pet memorial" and you'll see a number of such sites. Some will provide an artistic template to create a page for your pet. Other sites just let you upload pictures and comments. You can often browse other memorials and read their stories as well.

Some online memorial pages are connected with very helpful websites that provide articles, resources, chats, "webinars," and support groups for grieving pet-lovers. So check out what the rest of the site has to offer before you post your memorial. If you already have a website or a blog, you may choose to dedicate a page in tribute to your pet.

As always, keep your wits about you when putting out personal information on the Internet. Many of the online pet memorial sites are free to use, but you usually need to register first, and that would put your address on some e-mail sales lists. That might not be such a bad thing, but keep in mind that there are people who seek to take advantage of those who are grieving. Just be smart about it.

BENEFITING OTHERS

What would your pet want you to do as a memorial tribute? That's a hard question to answer, but it's worth thinking about. Web pages, shrines, poems, and key chains—they can all be a part of the healing-and-remembering process. But let's think in a completely different direction. Is there some incredibly loving, charitable act you could do in your pet's name that would truly make a difference?

Why not make a donation to an animal charity? The ASPCA, the most well known of these groups, is a long-standing non-profit organization with a good reputation. Or perhaps you'd like to support an organization that helps fund therapy animals for handicapped people or autistic children. If you need other ideas or don't have access to a computer to help in your research, call your local vet or shelter and ask if they can recommend a group.

Don't forget to think locally, too! There's probably an animal shelter in your county that's operating on a shoestring budget, and they need all the support they can get. They might even be able to use your old pet supplies. Some items, such as kitty litter or cage bedding or even half a bag of chow, would be welcome. Depending on the health of your pet and the circumstances of its death, other, more personal items such as toys, dishes, and grooming equipment may or may not be appropriate to donate. Call the shelter and review what you have with them.

Another way to memorialize your pet is to make a renewed effort to take care of yourself. After all, your pet would want you to be healthy and happy! Quit smoking. Start exercising. Restore contact with an estranged relative or former friend. Your desire to honor your pet's memory might give you the extra *oomph* you need to really accomplish the task.

LIVING, LOVING, AND ENJOYING

When you memorialize your pet in some way, you are "emotionally relocating" it. If you remember the task talk from chapter 4, you'll know that memorializing is the last of the four tasks we discussed. It's not the *removal* of the departed one from our consciousness but the *relocation*. We are taking it from our everyday consciousness and placing it into memory. Even as we focus on the pet for a service, an event, or a creative endeavor, we are saying goodbye. We are putting it in the past so we can move into the future.

It's also important to realize that the past fuels the future. The loves and losses of our history help to shape us, to make us ready for whatever we encounter in the days ahead. And this might turn out to be the most important legacy your pet leaves: *you.*

You can talk about loyalty, companionship, and the time your pet almost ate a whole ball of string, but what you're saying is that your pet helped you enjoy life. So, as you consider the most effective ways to honor your friend, here's the ultimate memorial: Be the person your pet helped you to be. Live. Love. Enjoy.

That might be pretty tough to remember right now, when you're hurting so much. Soon enough, there will come a time when life will float back within your reach. Grab it, taste it, and savor it.

In the name of the pet you've lost, open your heart again to love. Embrace the people around you, literally and figuratively. Put the needs of others ahead of your own. Do some good in the world.

And in those days of restoration, you will open yourself again to joy, real joy. Just the way your pet would have wanted.

Resources

WEBSITES

Find valuable articles, resources, and links at this site written by the Argus Institute at the Colorado State University Veterinary Teaching Hospital. **http://www.argusinstitute.colostate.edu**

The Association for Pet Loss and Bereavement runs this site, with information and connections. Check out the moderated chat rooms to talk through your issues. **aplb.org**

The Best Friends Animal Society is an animal-rescue charity. The site has some helpful resources and also offers memorial ideas. **bestfriends.org**

Chance's Spot is a nonprofit agency helping people with pet loss. The site contains links, articles, an online support group, and more. **chancesspot.org**

Search "pet loss" on this site and you'll find good articles broken down by type of animal. **peteducation.com/**

Petloss.com is a pet-loss support website that might prove helpful. **petloss.com**

This pet-loss support site contains a number of helpful articles along with ads from various pet-related businesses. **pet-loss.net**

Petplace.com boasts "over 15,000 vet-approved articles," including ones on pet loss. **petplace.com**

The University of California at Davis School of Veterinary Medicine's website contains plenty of information about pet care and pet loss. **vetmed.ucdavis.edu/ccab/petloss.html**

HOTLINES

The ASPCA offers a pet-loss hotline to help owners make a decision about euthanasia; come to terms with their grief; give advice on dealing with children, the elderly, or disabled individuals and the death of a pet; and more. Call **(877) GRIEF-10.**

Washington State University College of Veterinary Medicine students provide grief counseling at the pet-loss hotline. Messages can be left for their staff 24 hours a day. Note, however, that they cannot give medical advice. Phone: **(866) 266-8635**; e-mail: **plhl@vetmed. wsu.edu.**